The Pathological Liar
(the enemy)

Shemelia Henry

The Pathological Liar within (The Enemy)
© 2017 Shemelia Henry. All rights reserved.

No part of this book may be reproduced in any written, electroniac, recording or photocopying without written permission of the author. The exception would be in the case of brief quotations

The author can be contact at zariakc@gmail.com

ISBN-13: 978-1539086345

ISBN-10: 1539086348

Pathological Liar: Compulsive lying. Individuals may be aware that they are lying, or may believe that they are telling the truth.

Wikipedia

DEDICATION

To my mother, whom I love more than words could ever explain. Thank you mummy for always praying for me. Thank you for accepting the challenge when your name was called to raise me. I know it was not easy, being a single mother and unemployed for some of the years I was growing up. I appreciate that you never once allowed me to feel any of your struggles.

Thank you for being a woman of Poise and Grace. Throughout my life, you never once complained or said anything bad about my father but went out of your way to encourage a relationship between us. You taught me to respect him in spite of how I felt towards him at times.

Thank you for asking Yahweh for wisdom on how to raise me, because I know that your method was unconventional to most. You know it and I feel it, but it's proof that Yahweh gave you the grace to love me.

Emotionally, I'm not the easiest person in the world to deal with. My moods are all over the place — sometimes I'm up but most times I'm down. Derek Hough said it best: sometimes you hurt the ones you love the most, and I'm sorry for that. In spite of it all you just kept loving me.

Thank you for being a go-getter and for being the hardest working woman I know. Nothing or No one could hold you down.

Thank you for always coming whenever I call to save me from spiders and all other insects, even till this day!

You are a tomboy at heart; you're 52 years old and still can't resist climbing trees! We call ourselves two peas in a pod because we work so well together. Our go to song whenever we are doing something together is "Me and My Llama" from Sesame Street. Bottom line is — you are my Mummy first but thank you for also being my best friend!

I know granny named you Sharon and it's a beautiful name — just like you are, but thank you for answering to my special old fashioned nick name, Bertenel.

Thank you for answering to it in public, over and over again for many years, even though you promised you wouldn't, lol.

LOVE YOU MUMMY!

SPECIAL THANKS

Thank you to family and friends for all that you've allowed me to glean from your life journeys. Our moments together were crafted with precision by the Master of all things in heaven and on earth, and your obedience to Him to love me would not go unnoticed.

You all have affected my life with such profundity that it has made it impossible to find the words to express the gratitude that I feel. I love you all so much, and I know that I don't make that abundantly clear but I couldn't have become who I am today without your touch. I thank Yahweh for placing me in my mother's womb with the plans of having my life collide with yours. I pray that the peace of Yahweh will always encapsulate you and that you'll never doubt that the world is that much more amazing and rich because you were created. My humblest thank you.

CONTENTS

Page no.

Chapter I	**Unprepared/Unqualified**----------------------10
Chapter II	**Fear**..13
Chapter III	**It's Okay to Fall Just Don't Stay Down**..........15
Chapter IV	**Unhealthy Comparisons**...................................17
Chapter V	**Misunderstood**..20
Chapter VI	**Overly Critical**..23
Chapter VII	**Fear Part 2**..26
Chapter VIII	**Put On Hold/Forgotten**...................................30
Chapter IX	**Validation**...33
Chapter X	**Arrogance**..37
Chapter XI	**Delayed, Not Denied**......................................41
Chapter XII	**Deception**..49
Chapter XIII	**Legion**..55
Chapter XIV	**Identity**..58
Chapter XV	**Life Interrupted**...66
Chapter XVI	**Introspection**..70
Chapter XVII	**Depression, Suicide, Hope**..............................74

PREFACE

Hi, my name is Shemelia Henry. I'm 31 years old and I'm from Trinidad and Tobago in the West Indies. I'm writing this book by no strength of my own because truth be told, I feel extremely inadequate. I don't have a background in psychology and I don't know much about writing principles. But I'm going to share my story anyway, because what I do have is my experience with mental and emotional unbalance due to fear, worry, loneliness, guilt, envy, pride, self-doubt, lack of confidence, and hatred for myself and others.

As I share my story, I pray that it would not only connect with others but help at least one person. You may be feeling like you're in the wrong place. This life is not for you, you can't do anything right for any prolonged period of time, and you are now truly convinced that in spite of all of your good intentions and efforts, everyone else around you seems to be growing and evolving while you're still stuck at the starting line. Surely, you must be that one person that The Heavenly Father forgot about.

I want you to know that you're not alone and you're not crazy. We are just tired; tired from playing the role of the well put together, always smiling, happy, encouraging, selfless people that we portray. Believing that we have to be that way just so that we can barely be 'good enough.'

I don't have any tricks or secrets on how we can make ourselves better once and for all, but what you can expect is that I'm crying right along with you. Not because we are weak, but because we are in a process where the pressure is indescribable, and sometimes all we can do is cry. But cry with purpose, let our cry symbolise that we're no longer relying on our own strength but exchanged for Yahweh's divine orders and now it's just the sound of our humility. But there's one thing I know to be true — being humble requires a lot of effort. The enemy, as shallow as he is, will no doubt attack us — especially when we've made the decision to start doing the right thing. But our Father sees and hears our cries and He will reward our faithfulness.

I urge you to open-mindedly read this book because you'll find that there is no one sure way to reaching your destiny on this journey. The book is a bit sporadic and somewhat unedited because I wanted it to be authentic, so

I beg your forgiveness in advance for my lack of literary skills. I hope that one of the lessons from this book would be accepting the fact that even if you learnt something once, there is nothing wrong with having to relearn it; you must be willing to redefine yourself when necessary.

Chapter I
Unprepared/Unqualified

Writing doesn't come naturally to me — it's just one of those things that I say yes to out of sheer faith. I can't begin to express just how unprepared I feel because truth is, I'm still rummaging through the debris of my own life. How could I expect to gain the trust of others, to get them to step out of their boats and walk on the water when I myself have not even made it to dry land?

This could not be a more inconvenient time to be doing this, but The Heavenly Father can work in mysterious ways. In our finite minds, we think that we should start at point A, and then alphabetically proceed to point B through to Z, but Yahweh does things differently. He doesn't need perfect circumstances and may start us off at point A but since He is the author and finisher of our destiny, He could catapult us all the way to R, then back to G. He does what He wants when He wants and it may seem reckless at times, but His plans are always the best for us. If I have learnt nothing else from this process, I learnt to be silent — to watch, wait and trust. But in all honesty it wasn't easy.

Have you ever felt like you were held captive in a room and all the walls were made of one-way glass? That way you were privy to seeing everything around you, only to have it rendered unattainable? Well I have. In fact, it's a feeling I know all too well — being trapped in your own head, the torture of having all your senses for 'life' be aroused, only to be paralyzed by fear, doubt and feelings of insufficiency.

As a child, I've always had big dreams; that was never a problem for me, it was my norm. Like many kids, I had the empowerment of childlike faith. I was still the master of my thoughts — a female Pablo Picasso creating masterpieces on the canvas of my mind. My future was bright; there was no stopping me — until life happened.

Around the age of eighteen, I went from living happily with my dreams to a sudden feeling of being a complete stranger in the place I grew up, with the same people. I felt like I was in a coma for years and when I finally came out, I was thrust into a circus and I was the main act.

Because I felt so different from everyone else, the enemy became my confidante and told me negative things about myself. I mean, the facts were there but up until then it was not that big of a deal. Of course, he wasted no time, and worked double time to convince me that indeed they were a very big deal. He told me that I was fat and ugly, the gap in my teeth was too wide, my feet were too big, basically everything about my body was wrong, and when it came to my mental ability, well I was just simply unqualified. He was so great at reminding me that I had nothing worthy to offer this world; he was my closest friend and really stuck close to me over the years, making sure that no one else could befriend me. He fed me lies, always held my hand, allowed me to rest my head on his shoulders and took advantage of every weak moment that I had, making certain to tarnish any thread of worth that I may have felt.

He knew my two greatest desires were to be a wife and a mother. We had an intimate relationship, our lines of communication were always open and he whispered in my ear at the most opportune times. He told me every day that no man would ever love me the way he would, he reminded me daily that they wouldn't be able to handle all of my imperfections, and of course he never let me forget that I would never be good enough to be someone's mother. He didn't ask for much in return — only that I kept smiling, laughing and looking happy on the outside, as I looked at the world and people evolving, from the panoramic view of my glass room. I gave him all of my worries and cares to manage and he multiplied them and gave them back to me.

There was a time in my life when I felt like I only existed; there was no life in me. It was a constant struggle just to survive, and it was the worst kind of struggle because it's one thing to have a physical fight but it's a whole other thing when the fight is on the inside. It causes you to have untamed emotions, which affect your quality of life. It interferes with your relationships, putting your friends and family in unfair situations, because you're basically robbing them of forming any kind of a bond with you.

You can't make people feel loved if they don't love themselves. It is unjust to expect others to show you your worth, and it's not possible. Untamed emotions will drain you more than physical labour ever could. They will rob you of precious time, time that you could spend with loved ones, and they dis tract you from being present in the moment, where you can produce pleasant memories. Untamed emotions are so unpredictable and overwhelming that after a while they start to break you down and when you don't deal with them, before you know it you become numb.

The liar within forces you to ask a lot of questions. This can be a good thing but it can also be a double-edged sword when the conflict comes and you ask those questions but allow your preconceived notions to take precedent over the truth. That's what I did — which only strengthened my belief that I was a less than average person with nothing to contribute to this life.

Chapter II
FEAR

Fear makes it easier to respond to the familiar voice rather than a more peculiar voice, even though there is life and endless possibilities coming from it.

―――

Fear paralyzed me. To be honest, even the very prospect of writing this book scared me and I thought of 99 reasons why I shouldn't. Fear had a very prominent place in my life, and I didn't even realize it. Looking back, I now see how I self-sabotaged every area of my life because of fear. Fear can manifest in many different ways and you have to learn how to detect it. I'm still bombarded with fear on a daily basis but I know that the only way to fight is with the truth of The Father — that's what The Word is for. I don't always know what to pray for or how to pray so I speak the word when in this situation.

2nd Timothy 1:7 NKJV "For Yahweh has not given us a spirit of fear, but of power and of love and of a sound mind."

I will be real with you. It isn't easy to say those words, let alone believe it; especially when every fibre of your being is shouting to run for cover. Nevertheless, I have to keep on saying it, even if it doesn't look or feel like anything is happening. I have to have faith that it is. I can't quit.

I just want to encourage those of you, who are sick and tired of being sick and tired — use this low point in your life as the catalyst to motivate yourself to push forward.

―――

Believe it or not — it's only when you have maxed out your limited resources then you become creative.

If you know that you have a problem but you just can't figure out exactly what it is yet, that's still a very good place to start. Just make the first step in faith and Yahweh will start shining light on some things in your life that are retarding your growth. I encourage you to take the necessary steps to becoming who Yahweh created you to be, but remember it starts with you making the first step. It's daunting I know, but be deliberate and consistent.

Trust me, I know what it feels like to be afflicted and to be in a fight with something that is not physical. I would much rather have a full out fist fight and have someone hit me! At least I would know what or who was causing my pain. Fear is like a cancer eating away at your dignity, your self-worth, and your perspective on life. It reduces you to nought; it steals your quality of life and fills you with indescribable pain. It takes forceful effort to get out of those trenches and I know what it's like to open my eyes on mornings and give thanks for Yahweh having spared my life — only because those words are on autopilot.

I am still on my journey. I am not where I want to be but thank Yahweh I'm not where I used to be. On some days I have to arm myself with more spiritual armour than others but by Yahweh's grace, I have the strength for my battles and he'll do the same for you. We just have to keep pressing forward, doing the right thing, even when we are not seeing the fruits of our labour. In that obscure place, the potency of who we really are would be extracted and developed.

I laugh at those words, because this faith walk is hard. That's the truth. I am enduring difficulty as I've never experienced before. And I'm baffled, because although I'm going through some stretching in my life, I have this fervent desire to pen my experiences with the purest intentions that it would breathe hope into someone else's situation. It's as though I am two different people, I know I should not doubt Yahweh but how could I not marvel? When I attended school, I detested writing essays and judging by the content of my work, it showed. Even now, I can't tell you how many times I hit the auto spell correct key, my attempt at spelling is almost laughable. In the end, I guess all I can say is press me to improve Yah.

Fear is only a trick of the enemy to keep you limited,
to cloud your judgment, to alter your perspective.

Yielding to fear makes you a victim and uses you as a puppet.

IT'S ONLY A TEST   IT'S ONLY A TEST   IT'S ONLY A TEST

Chapter III
IT'S OKAY TO FALL — JUST DON'T STAY DOWN!

I have been a puppet of the enemy for most of my life. My moods were based on the vicissitudes of my circumstances. They were tarnishing my character; I was so unpredictable, you never knew which side of me would show up. As I wrote this book, I was forced to take a hard look at my life. Even though I was spending most of my time highlighting my flaws, I hated having to admit that I have bad habits (crutches). We all develop them to be able to cope with life, but for some reason Yahweh exposed mine. I guess you can say I was openly convicted but I am not a finished product. I am still a work in progress, as we all are.

Saturday 13 September, 2014

It's 2:39 p.m. and I just got home from bible service with the family. We gather every week and usually start by giving praise to Yah through song, then we go into the scriptures, but today things went a bit differently for me. About half an hour into the service, I got distracted. My mind was no longer on The Creator, and that provided a space for the enemy to walk right in and make himself at home in my head. For the next two hours, I was just angry; angry with myself, my life and my family. In the moment I validated my attitude, but looking back now I realise it was absolutely absurd. There was no feasible explanation for the shift in my emotions, no one did anything to me, and nothing happened. I just felt angry and kept on getting angrier to the point of tears. Thinking about it now, I guess the only explanation I could come up with is that I was angry because they seemed happy and I wasn't.

Bottom line is, today I fell and that's okay. In fact, I am prepared to fall again and get a lot more bruises but I pray that it's not in the same place every time. Whenever I fall, I have to remember that it's okay. The truth of the matter isn't a surprise to Yahweh, it's a surprise to me. The real test is whether I succumb to my injuries or pick myself up, dust myself off, and keep pressing forward, collecting the data so that I can be better equipped for the next test. Because the next test will most likely be tougher than the last — just as Matthew 12:45 NKJV says, "Then he goes and takes with him seven other spirits more wicked than himself, and they enter and dwell there: and the last state of that man is worse than the first."

This verse scares me, but it should serve as a warning to make not only me, but also you aware to keep our guard up. This is not the time to be complacent! The 43rd verse of that same chapter says, "When an unclean spirit goes out of a man, he goes through dry places, seeking rest, and finds none." Dry places as they pertain to our life, are those areas where we are not being the best expression of who Yahweh created us to be.

Do I have any dry places in my life? Sure I do. Am I proud of them? No, I'm not. Truth is, it's embarrassing but because I have chosen to follow my convictions and write this book, I am talking about the areas which affect me most, and one of them is my propensity for unhealthy comparisons.

Chapter IV
UNHEALTHY COMPARISONS

I started running life's race in my lane and somehow, other people's races distracted me. I have spent so much time focusing and recognizing what other people had, that I lost total sense of what I have. That internal voice of deception became so loud and clear, I felt that I was living in a room of emptiness and the space of nothingness was in me.

My self-esteem, if measured on a scale from 1 to 10 would have read -1. I questioned my worth and my purpose almost every waking moment of every day. I compared myself to every person I met. I saw their beauty, I saw their talents, and recognized their potential, but then I would look at myself and only find faults. It's one thing to compare yourself to people in general but it is downright inexcusable to compare yourself to your own mother, especially a mother like mine. I am her only child and she continues to do everything for me. I am her baby, and she is the one person I know for sure loves me unconditionally.

Yet I couldn't have an innocent, uninterrupted conversation with her without wishing I was my mother's physical size. We'd be having a conversation and in my head I'd be comparing her waistline with mine, the size of her arms and legs with mine. In fact, I've said it out loud on numerous occasions, "I wish I was your size." I constantly compared myself to an elephant and I knew it pained her that her child was not happy but in those moments I wasn't disciplined enough to keep my feelings to myself, and that disregard for other people's feelings became a part of my character. I felt like I had nothing to lose, I needed everyone to feel at least one drop of the pain I was feeling.

I also mastered the art of sarcasm. I was so judgmental that I waited for people to make a mistake so that I could magnify it in my mind just to feel good about myself; I was self-medicating on people's failures. I was so insecure that it was almost impossible to compliment others because I felt like it was taking away from what I didn't have.

Self-Realisation plays a critical role in our purpose and ultimately our destiny because we all have gifts and talents that are flowing in abundance. But the enemy blinds us. He keeps us so captivated by everyone else's talents that we forget that in this "spiritual body" everyone has a function. We always want what is not ours, rather than learn to work with what we have.

I am so grateful that my seed has started to germinate. I am far from being a blossoming tree but I am getting there. My roots drink from Yahweh's life giving waters every day and that has fortified me. My prayer is that you too would know that you have seeds of greatness inside of you. All it takes is for you to get into Yahweh's word and allow it to saturate you. I also pray that the need to be validated by 'MAN' will be eradicated, and that our ears will hear only the voice of The Father and that His love and grace will be unmistakable, so we may boldly walk in the part that He has charted out for us.

My life starts when I could look at other people and see them, rather than a reflection of who I am not.

"Rejoice with those who rejoice" Romans 12:15 NKJV. What do you do when something you were longing for comes through for another? You take part in celebrating it, but you're not the guest of honour at the party.

It's amazing that no matter how many tests I have taken in the different areas of my life, there is always this recurring question about the maturity of my selflessness. Perhaps He who knows my mind is not satisfied with my past answers and keeps giving me opportunities so that I could eventually answer correctly, and not just pay lip service by going through the motions.

I did a pretty OK job at pretending to actually care about the accomplishments of others, and while it was acceptable to everyone else, it wasn't to Him. In the long run, He knew that my way wouldn't be hurting anyone but myself. It took me a very long time to realize that. Yahweh is masterful and that was one of his strategies for moulding me into the person He wants me to become. He kept putting me in situations where I had to be happy for others, even though I didn't like it. It has been a very slow process but I'm definitely getting better.

Yahweh's ways are not our ways and as I reflect on life, I notice a pattern. As human beings, we tend to highlight our strengths. We nurture them, advertise them, and focus on them. But the amazing thing about Yahweh is that He is interested in our weaknesses, because He gets to show us how strong He is teaching us how to overcome and be made stronger.

I believe that my purpose lies just under the surface of my problems. The only drawback is that sometimes I feel like my surface is a bit too thick. The paradox of my life is that I have perceived what causes me to do the things that I do and I'm not proud of it, but I still subconsciously and sometimes consciously allow it to control me.

I'm irritably learning that timing is everything, and as uncomfortable as it is being on the potter's wheel, I take solace in the fact that He is the greatest at what He does.

Society has taught us to judge based on facts, but Yahweh does things differently. He sees the 'Truth.' He knows our potential, and I have to remind myself constantly that I am already the guest of honour at the most elite party — Yahweh's party! And you are too. I know that you are weary; I know that you are bombarded with thoughts of unbelief that you will ever receive your promise. But from one 'outpatient' to another, I urge you to consider the distance that you have already travelled. Don't give up now.

It may seem like your purpose in life is taking a lifetime to come to fruition, but keep in mind that a gift given too soon is not a gift at all. We are being strengthened to be able to withstand the weight of our blessings, just as it is written in Isaiah 40:31 NKJV, *"But those who wait on Yahweh shall renew their strength; they shall mount up with wings like eagles; they shall run, and not be weary; they shall walk, and not faint."*

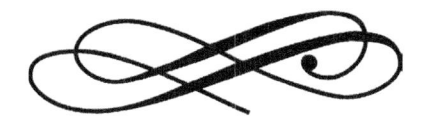

Chapter V
MISUNDERSTOOD

Feeling misunderstood is probably one of the most frustrating feelings that I've ever felt. People, including family and friends, as well intentioned as they are, sometimes say the most uninformed, insensitive things to you. I know that people are entitled to their own opinion but it doesn't make it any easier to listen to others blabbing about things that they do not understand.

I especially don't like it when they tell me how I should be feeling based on their assumptions. For example, they would say things like, "Why are you worried about your size? I've seen women bigger than you." Or, "Yes you're big but at least you have a good shape and a pretty face." I guess I shouldn't be angry with anyone for making those statements because it's unreasonable to expect them to be sensitive to the things that I've decorated with callus.

I spun a web around myself and I felt trapped. I became tired of pretending that everything was fine but on the other hand, I was always so concerned about hurting people's feelings, that I'd start debating back and forth in my head whether or not I should speak up. Most times, I opted to be misunderstood and left in the turmoil of my own mental incarceration, which inevitably became a problem.

The mistake was mine because rather than saying then and there how I felt, I expected family and friends to have a clearer understanding of what was wrong with me, and not give cookie cutter responses. I expected them to live up to my unrealistic expectations of being my personally assigned ego fluffers, psychotherapists, or somehow elevate themselves to the status of Yahweh and fix me, which was unfair because I set them up for failure. How could they ever have a genuine relationship with me when I was being dishonest with them and disregarding myself in the process?

Being vulnerable took a lot of courage; well it certainly did for me and was extremely difficult. I needed to feel in control and had no desire to let my guard down and show my emotions because people would see me as a 'softy' or 'needy.' I felt in control when I was acting composed, even though everything else in my life was falling apart at the seams.

The main reason for wanting to appear composed and reputable was to feel better about myself in front of people. Also, for some unknown reason, people would confide in me and tell me their problems, which made me feel like less of a failure at life.

I was a disingenuous opportunist mask in compassion. I gave advice, I encouraged, I made people laugh. I saw their lives change in amazing ways but it was not about them, it was about me. I lived to hear "Thank You," "What you're saying is right." I desperately needed to hear those affirmations.

Truth is, no one on earth could ever completely understand another person. We are all complex and this complexity is our commonality. As we meander our way through life, we may stumble across someone who is able to relate to us on various levels. So much so, that it would create a safe place for us to feel comfortable to expose the diamond buried beneath our rough, and if that is the case, we should count our blessings.

But my disclaimer is: do not let that be our main source of validation; there is a season for everything in life, including human resources. There will come a time when humans have limited resources and they will disappoint us. They may not do it on purpose but that's just the way the cookie crumbles. However, Yahweh is omniscient and never fails us; we should take refuge in Him. We have to accept that not everyone is going to understand what we're going through. Of course, it would be great if they did but that would be a fairy tale. My point is, it's not a one way street. They also have their lives and their problems so we shouldn't be so hard on them, and at least consider opening up more.

Vulnerability is strength. It breaks the silence and allows you to breathe, but at all times, pray for divine connections.

**Eternal Father,
I am sorry for the times I thought I was a victim,
and I'm sorry that I victimized others in their time of weakness.
I thank you for renewing me. I thank you for removing
the clutter from my mind so that I can clearly see the works**

**of the enemy in my life. I thank you for turning around
what the enemy meant for bad to good.
Thank you for not allowing my experiences to be wasted.
Thank you for the strength to take my pain and use it
as fuel to help others. Thank you for birthing
Empathy, Honesty and Love through by brokenness.**

I shared that prayer because I'm truly sorry for my actions. It gave me pleasure to criticize people that I knew — never to their face, but to someone else in hopes that they would agree with me. It made me feel better about myself. I wrote it so that you can say it too, if you feel any convictions about having said or done anything to hurt someone else during your time of hurt.

Chapter VI
OVERLY CRITICAL

If you're anything like I was, nothing you could do or say is ever good enough. Even when someone pays you a compliment, you find a way to dissolve it. Isn't it ironic that the one thing we are good at is self-degradation? I used every opportunity to magnify my weaknesses and insecurities but felt offended when people noticed them. It is imperative to know that whatever you think about yourself you manifest, and because I maintained the train of thought that I was no good, it wasn't long before I found myself feeling utterly lost and incomplete.

It's sad to say but I called that negative space home for the past few years of my life. Every morning as I opened my eyes until I closed them at night, I listened to the same record over and over, "Shemelia, you are an error; you're incomplete." I felt so obsolete and fearful. I was like a drug addict, who kept searching for stronger and stronger drugs to numb my pain, my drug was rejoicing over other people's failures. But, after a while, it no longer worked for me; it stopped being the distraction and comfort that I needed it to be.

I felt hopeless, and gave up altogether, which turned out to be a blessing in disguise because I was no longer self-medicating. Reaching rock bottom made me the perfect candidate to be helped and The Father stepped in. During that time, I heard someone say, "Learned hopelessness can be unlearned." That was profound for me because up until that time, I had no idea that my thoughts played such a huge role in perpetuating my feelings of dispensability.

2nd Corinthians 12:9 NKJV *"My grace is sufficient for thee; for my strength is made perfect in weakness."*

I never understood how closely linked the spiritual world was to the physical world. I never knew that purpose could open me up to such tumultuous, incomprehensible strife. I didn't know why I was always being attacked until I understood that my life was the way it was because I was wasting my energy responding to threats by Satan. I spent all my time reacting to fear; I went to bed bed scared and tired, and woke up scared and tired. I cried scared and tired, I laughed scared and tired. Before I could take care of one problem, another one popped up. It was a never-ending cycle of trying to conquer a giant that was not mine to conquer.

Blessed was the day when wisdom intervened in my life. I always knew of Yahweh but I didn't have a personal relationship with Him until I surrendered and asked Him to do what only He could do. I had nothing to lose, so at age 27, I gave Yahweh the invitation to come into my life. It was the best but toughest decision I ever made.

I wish I could say that from that day until now, life has just been wonderful but it's been tough. However, the difference between the old me and the redeemed me (Psalm 107:2 NKJV), is that I'm wearing the helmet of salvation (Ephesians 6:17 NKJV), and the full armour of Yahweh (Ephesians 6:11 NKJV). Now, when I start to feel intimidated or fearful, I fire back because I know that He that is in me is greater than he that is in the world (1st John 4:4 NKJV).

It is empowering to know that the choice is mine. I can either focus on who I was or who I am, and I have to constantly and affirmatively choose truth. That choice is also given to you and choosing to believe the truth in this world that is saturated with so many lies is not going to be easy but it can be done. Remember, it's not a one-time thing.

Believe me when I say that at first it's going to be downright embarrassing and borderline insane to look at the 'facts' of your life and spew all over it, because you choose to believe that the plans your Heavenly Father have for your life hold no resemblance to your temporary position. Stand on the promises of Yahweh.

I understood how risky it was to focus on what was happening in my present situation. Nothing changed physically but I refused to allow my circumstances to hinder me from dreaming and I am thankful that I didn't give up. When I felt discouraged, my dreams for something greater and the knowledge of my Heavenly Father being the master of turning the impossible into possible, kept me walking towards my purpose.

There came a time when I had to decide that in order to truly invest and trust in Yahweh's promises, even when everything in my life appeared to be at a standstill, I had to be willing to look crazy, act crazy, be called crazy and take it as a compliment. The only option was to start declaring it and acting like I already received it. If I didn't, 'exceptionalism' was not for me but I am exceptional so I chose to believe in Yahweh for the extraordinary.

Chapter VII
FEAR PART 2

Fear is debilitating and has become an epidemic. We don't really talk about it; we either isolate ourselves or over compensate, afraid to admit that our minds are being molested.

We are threatened with something on a daily basis, which the enemy holds over our heads and uses to manipulate us. For me, it's several things, but the one he uses most often is the fear of illness. No one likes to be sick but for me it's on a whole other level. I remember when it started and how it started.

I was always healthy except for the flu here and there, nothing to shout about until I was 19 years of age. One day I went to the gym, had a good workout and came home. When I went into the shower, I started feeling some discomfort and by that night, I was in full-blown pain. I was later told that I had haemorrhoids. The pain was terrible, but that was the easiest part. What really flipped my world upside down was that my aunt had the same thing and needed surgery for it. The fear was insurmountable but after an embarrassing trip to the doctor and a few suppositories, I was back to good health.

Although the flare up only lasted for two weeks, the trauma never left, and I began having anxiety. All it took was for someone to mention the symptoms of any disease and I would automatically start experiencing those exact symptoms, or so I would think. I worried day and night about getting sick but not nearly half as much as I worried about my mother getting sick and possibly dying. I monitored her every movement as much as I was able to and I was on her like a drill sergeant about what she ate.

The term used to describe someone like me is a hypochondriac but I try not to call myself that as I know the power of words, and I refuse to give more power to the forces that are fighting against me. People who know me would be surprised at the severity of this fear, as I'm a well-known alternative medicine advocate. In fact, a group of my friends call me the 'tea lady' because I'm always drinking and talking about various teas, including herbs and green juices, and taking the preventative route. This is a good thing but often times the line is blurred between trying to keep my immune system boosted and clear of prescription drugs, and worrying that if I don't take matters into my own hands, I'll contract every illness there is.

Fear causes you to hallucinate. You see things that aren't there, you feel things that aren't true. Like this autoimmune disease that my imagination has been attacking me with since I got sick. If that isn't bad enough, I'm not only worried about getting sick again, but I've been threatened with what is possible. My mind games booked my paranoia for the future and I was convinced that one day I would be stricken with some disease.

The feeling of fear is real but the thing feared is often not as scary. Even though my mind tries to convince me otherwise, I have to keep telling myself that it's not true. It's not an easy road because sometimes I hear of someone who is sick, especially someone that I know, and the anxiety gets the better of me. However, my state of mind is a lot more stable now, thanks to endless prayers because trying to fight that giant on my own is nothing short of impossible.

Fear makes you exhaust way more time and energy than you have to. It places you in the driver's seat without a license. Even if you think you can drive, you won't get very far without the law catching up with you.

I had to learn this hard lesson — it's not all up to me to make everything right for myself. I have a Father who loves me so much, and is just waiting for me to give Him my messes. Remember when we were children, and we would give something we were eating and didn't want any more to our parents and they would finish it? Or, we would drink from them and some of our food would fall into their cup but our parents still drank from it anyway (Gross I know, but hear me out)? Well, our Heavenly Father would do just like that, only magnified many more times. He is willing to be invited into our most complicated situations to clean up our messes, without judging us.

There are so many fearful strongholds in my life. Every time I think that I have conquered one thing, there is something else trying to get me to believe the voices in my head. They tell me that I'm just one big mistake, that this world is too scary, so I better stay crippled, sorry I meant "safe." I do wonder at times if I'll make it out of this, because the fear is so real. It's a lie but it feels real. When fear engulfs you, it does its most destructive work. It isolates you, and makes you separate yourself from people because you think that they'll never understand what you're going through. And when what's on the outside is terrifying, you start to internalize everything. The enemy thrives on this because he knows that if he can get you to believe that all you're doing is protecting yourself, he'll see to it that you fight anything that threatens your "safe" place. Little do you know at the time that your safe place is his dungeon.

I'm still fighting, but now I'm fighting all the lies that I so strongly believed for too long. It's hard — trying to fight what were my allies for years, but I'm fighting anyway. I have no intentions of going down without getting in some punches!

I don't know what your barriers are but I want you to know that you don't have to fight alone. I want to remind you that the magnitude of your troubles is an excellent gauge as to how high you are meant to soar. Don't be defeated by the things that are only there to extract the elixir given to you when you were placed in your mother's womb. It's possibly going to be the hardest thing that you'll ever have to do (and I'm sorry for being so dark) but prepare yourself to be battered and bruised. Don't ever let your guard down, because that's the thing about fear — it is so weak that it only attacks you when you are vulnerable. It always appears bigger than it really is, it doesn't play fair, and it comes upon us from a higher vantage point when we are buried in our insecurities. Let us do like King David and slay the beast in our lives, using the written word as the jawbone. Let us use the written word to paint over the tainted images we have of ourselves, to speak words of truth and upliftment over our lives, and as a protective garment to shield ourselves from the toxic lies that the enemy will try to contaminate our minds with.

2nd Corinthians 10:3-6 NKJV

"For though we walk in the flesh, we do not war after to the flesh: (For the weapons of our warfare are not carnal, but mighty through Yahweh to the pulling down of strong holds;) Casting down imaginations, and every high thing that exalteth itself against the knowledge of Yahweh, and bringing into captivity every thought to the obedience of Yahsuah; And having in a readiness to revenge all disobedience, when your obedience is fulfilled."

2nd Timothy 1:7 NKJV

"For Yahweh hath not given us the spirit of fear; but of power, and of love, and of a sound mind."

Chapter VIII
PUT ON HOLD/FORGOTTEN

Have you ever thrown a batch of laundry into the tub and a small article of clothing fell out but instead of picking it up, you left it for later and forgot all about it? Well that's how I feel sometimes; like that disregarded piece of clothing, like Yahweh forgot about me. My life seems so monotonous — the same old ugly shade of grey for many years.

Also, it's hard to see people having victorious moments everywhere I turn, especially flaunting their accomplishments via social media.

I know that in order to get from one level to the next I have to be tested, and I have no problem with that. Life hasn't blindsided me by giving me tests; in fact I was expecting them. But, the successes of those who haven't been nearly as faithful or sacrificial as I've been has me questioning the requirements to be shown favour. I know how that must sound, especially from someone who knows what the bible says about judging and coveting but to be honest, I would be breaking another commandment by lying or pretending that those thoughts don't make laps in my head.

The very thought of celebrating other people's victories and triumphs is a major source of discontentment for me, because it's never when I'm having a similar experience but always when I'm in the perils of my own living hell that I have to put on a smile. It's exhausting. I know that I should not judge but excuse me for being human because I do. It's not something that I'm proud of but it's the truth.

It just seems that from where I stand, everyone's life is full of colour, and I'm not saying that they don't have grey days but at least there is alternation; there are different seasons in their lives, but my life feels stuck in one season. I feel so predictable. One day I heard someone say, "Don't get mad at other people because you allow your timidity to stop you from being like Peter and stepping out onto the water." I thought that I was depressed but now I know that I'm oppressed by my own insecurities. I searched tirelessly for reasons and persons other than myself to blame for the dysfunctions in my life, but that search proved to be ineffective.

Matthew 14:29 NKJV

*"So he said, "come". And when Peter had
come down out of the boat, he walked
on the water, to go to Yahsuah."*

I know that I cannot and will not be victorious at anything if I only lean on my own strength, but my willingness and my effort is critical. I keep waiting for perfect situations but Yahweh doesn't call the equipped, he equips who he calls. For far too long I have allowed the fear of failure to stop me from trying, but something has to change. I can't afford to continue short changing myself.

It's not right for me to be angry and jealous of others for being brave enough to leap, but the enemy sometimes whispers, "Their circumstances are different from yours. They're not dealing with half of what you have to deal with, which makes their process a lot easier than yours. What they're risking is miniscule compared to what you're risking."

I focus so much on the award ceremonies of people's lives that I disregard what it takes for them to reach that stage. All I see are the times they leap and soar, and the liar within me conveniently nullifies the many more times that they leaped and fell but were courageous enough to get back up and try again.

The truth is, there will be times when life is going to demand something from me that in the moment, will feel like it's going to kill me; or that I think is unfair, but I have to do it anyway. If my desire is to someday receive all that I have been promised, I must act when called to. It's hard, really hard to do, but I can do all things through the power and strength of The Father. He is not going to ask something of me that wouldn't be beneficial. It doesn't matter what He requires of me but sometimes I hate The Process and if I had my way, I'd skip so many stages but I can't. This is where my faith has to be put to the test, and I don't have any other choice but to remain steadfast. Yahweh is faithful and delivers to those who obey Him.

Psalms 37:23 NKJV

*"The steps of a good man are ordered by Yahweh,
and he delights in his way."*

Proverbs 13:12 NKJV

*"Hope deferred makes the heart sick,
but when the desire comes, it is a tree of life."*

Chapter IX
VALIDATION

Monday 02 February, 2015

It's 10:02 p.m. and we just got home from fitness camp. I did an intense core workout and I was very proud of myself. I had good form, felt the burn, did better than the prior class, and I was really happy. After the session, we had to do an evaluation to get started in the right direction for our fitness journey. Everything was going well until coach said, "Wow Sharon, you're really losing that weight, it shows in your face," and her husband echoed, "Yes, yes, she's losing it."

The logical, compassionate side of me felt so happy for my mother. After all, I knew what hard work she was putting in, but that didn't stop the insecure, broken pieces of me from feeling instantly jealous and disappointed. I am really tempted to quit now, because I worked just as hard as she did, but apparently my weight loss wasn't significant enough to be noticed. I feel terrible for thinking this way. I love my mother and I'm happy for her progress. I'm just really frustrated that my efforts went unnoticed. Trying to lose weight is not easy at all, especially for me who at my heaviest weighed 350 lbs. I'm currently 242.2 lbs. which is a great accomplishment for most, but I'm having a lot of difficulties celebrating that.

Friday 06 February, 2015

I took a few days off from writing because I needed time to sort through some emotions. I had to acquiesce to the truth that I am desperate for approval from others and it's more severe than I thought it was. I can't believe I reached that extreme point where I was actually envious of my own mother, which is inexcusable.

I'm so heavily dependent on other people's opinion for my validation. It took me thirty years to realize that I was trying to live my life based on how I was perceived by others, which was way too much power to give to people. It was simply disappointing, unfulfilling and frustrating. As far back as I can remember, I have valued the opinions of others more than that of myself, I lived my life at the mercy of others.

I spent my days as a chameleon, trying to become what I thought would be acceptable. The problem is that I was left exhausted and confused. I thought my problem was on the outside, but it wasn't. It was in my mind. And it's sad to know that I wasted so much of my life by not understanding my worth. Rather than demanding that people work for my worth, I cut costs by giving them counterfeits of myself. What's more sad is that I allowed the background noise to drown out that soft, still voice of The Father's unconditional love.

I completely disregarded all the seemingly 'small blessings' in my life by waiting on tangible blessings, or what I called 'big blessings.' Those things that would capture the attention of others so that they would acknowledge me — only then would they be good enough for me to believe and appreciate. But even that feeling of gratification would not last long. As soon as the attention was off me, I would go back to feeling insufficient and discontented.

It's interesting how the inspiration for writing this book comes. Presently, the only person who knows that I'm writing this book is my mother. I told her that I have to take it layer by layer and by that, I mean the only time I write is when I'm at the point of hopelessness. When I start to feel extremely overwhelmed about any situation, I'm left with no other choice but to tune out the noise in my own head, thus allowing the Heavenly Father to show me why He is not removing some of the obstacles in my way. Honestly, as much as I understand the end result, I utterly dislike the means because it doesn't feel good. It's my default setting to ask, "Why me?" which I revert to very regularly. The ironic thing is, I don't know why I keep asking that question because I seldom like the answers I get. The responses always leave me feeling exposed, vulnerable, and at times, reluctantly humbled.

I'm basically sorting through my dirty laundry and because of that, I wonder if this is even meant to be a book at all, or only a journal. I'm really having a fight in my mind as to whether or not I want this book published. What if no one reads my book? What if they read my book and they judge me? What am I going to do then?

Those questions are always circulating in my head. I wish they didn't but they do and it's up to me to identify the deceptive voice in my head and ignore them anyway. The sooner I stop focusing on what others have, the faster I'll realize that I have all that I need in me to blaze my own trail. There is no wrong or right way, because every turn takes me to a new level in my learning. I just have to gather the treasures along the way and learn to love and accept those treasures in me so that I can love and accept the treasures in others. I have to learn how to cheerfully celebrate and magnify other people's victories, which in itself will be a validation of who I am as a child of Yahweh.

I realize that I can't force people to love me, and now that I've had some time to really think about it, the reality is, people loving me is not the problem. I am loved. I have an amazing, close group of people in my life that I get to call my family and friends and I know that they love me. The real question is, "Do I love me?"

The greatest fight of my life is to love myself. I am my own bully. I don't give anyone much of a chance to disfigure me, I do all the scarring on my own. To answer the question honestly, almost every day I have to fight the urge to devalue myself, but my victory is that I'm still fighting.

I tried almost every hack there is to 'learn to love myself.' As I woke on mornings, I would force myself to say "You are beautiful," or I'd stand in front of the mirror saying "You are slim," or "You are full of joy." I've even plastered post-its all over my walls to act as positive reminders of how beautiful I am, but that didn't work for me. I'm not saying that it wouldn't work for you because everyone is different. It was discouraging but I'm holding on to my belief that everyone must have their own unique encounter with Yahweh, and I wanted mine.

It's taken me a long time to understand and accept that if I was to have any chance of contentment in this lifetime, I would have to forfeit my plans and everybody else's plans for my life, and trust Yahweh. That is not easy for me to do. The best way to describe it is like sitting in the passenger seat with a really terrible driver who slows down when he should be going fast or speeds up when he should be slowing down. Or, he just slams on the brakes at the most inopportune time and all you want to do is shout, "What are you doing?!" And even though you may be traumatised by then and on the verge of a nervous breakdown, you still arrive at your destination with the breath of life in you, which is a sure sign that anything is possible. Well, that's the way it is with Yahweh!

So, I'm buckled in for the ride and I'm taking it one step at a time. My plan of action is to dig deep, looking for the things that I love about myself and magnify them. I love that I'm very strong willed; really, you'd have a definite fight on your hands trying to get me to do something that I don't want to do. And I'm proud of myself for not giving up when I really wanted too. Don't get me wrong, I'm not conceited by any stretch of the imagination. I just had to look for the things that were not obvious about myself to start with, because when it came to the physical, I couldn't see anything to like, much less to love.

Thank you ever near, ever-dear Father
for loving me so strongly, even when I thought
I didn't deserve to be loved. I now see a glimmer
of what you and everyone else around me can see.
I have so much hope for your finished work in me.
I'm nowhere near completion but your scripture
told me about your plans and I know that you do not lie.
I stand in awe of your constant, renewing work in me,
and of the deposits of humility and compassion
that you've stirring up in me for other hurting souls.
Thank you for cleaning my lens so that I can see
all the majestic colours of hope, grace, and love in my life.

Chapter X
ARROGANCE

Thursday 26 February, 2015.

My mother and I had one of our many talks today, and the topic of peer pressure came up. I must admit that in some chauvinistic way I enjoyed that topic. I felt large and in charge, I was so sure of myself. I was on a roll and it felt so good, speaking with such authority. If I had my way, I would have spoken about it for hours, dissecting and judging people because they fell into peer pressure.

A few hours later, I read the biography of a certain woman who thanked Yahweh for giving her the strength to overcome her addiction. She wrote of the many times she tried to get rid of her addiction and failed, and how looking back on her journey, she now understood why there were so many failures in her life. She finally realized that she was unsuccessful because she was trying to do it on her own. When I read that, a light went on. I realized why it was so easy for me to cast judgment on others for succumbing to peer pressure. It was an area of my life where I had strength.

I am usually very opinionated, but this morning I was opinionated to the point of boastfulness. I was so busy judging people because they sinned differently from me.

I realise now that I allowed the enemy to creep into my life again and fertilise the seed of pride. The terrifying thing was thinking about how long that seed had been planted before I was convicted. It's so scary to think about how you can be doing something so wrong for so long and not care, or unaware of the damage that you may be causing.

In my weakened and vulnerable state of mind, I was so desperate to be strong that I latched onto the first crutch that presented itself without doing the necessary background check.

Arrogance portrayed at its best, is Pride.

I condemned anyone who fell into peer pressure. I was proud of saying that there wasn't a soul on this earth who could take me anywhere I didn't want to go, or change my mind from doing what I wanted to do.

To be clear, that was a correct statement because no one is responsible for my destruction but me. However, the discrepancy has to do with how I said it. I had venom when I spoke, almost as though I was angry with the people who had fallen into the snares of peer pressure.

But as I reflected on my actions, I couldn't help but conclude that I was not really angry with anyone but myself. Under all of my hostility, I must have subconsciously known that I had already given into Satan's influence. And of course, his typical way of doing things is to shine the light on people's faults and magnify them which made me the perfect candidate for the job.

Satan was working overtime on my mind, but I thank The Almighty for his saving grace; for convicting me and giving me the strength to yield to my conviction so that I would stop collecting spiritual bodies.

I guess that the one positive of me being so consumed with comparing myself to others and not feeling like I measured up, is that it kept me from falling in with the crowd.

Proverbs 4: 23-27 NKJV

"Keep your heart with all diligence;
for out of it spring the issues of life.
Put away from you a deceitful mouth,
and put perverse lips far from you.
Let your eyes look straight ahead,
and your eyelids look right before you.
Ponder the path of your feet,
and let all your ways be established.
Do not turn to the right or the left;
remove your foot from evil."

Oftentimes, when I see people struggling in an area where I have discipline, it's easy for me to judge them. It's intensified especially when it's a loved one, and most of the time I mean well but my delivery compromises the effect. I have to reprogram myself to strive toward showing meekness and kindness to others. Meekness is not weakness; it is strength under control. The main objective should always be for the upliftment, encouragement and betterment of the other person. The secret to achieving all of this is through love, because love casts away all guilt, worry, and fear. It provides a space for you to stumble and fall without being judged, but it also extends a helping hand up.

I've been a recipient of this amazing love time and time again. One example is my battle with weight. I tried so many diets and exercise programs throughout the years but none of them worked, all because my desire to lose weight wasn't as strong as the pain of the familiar. Losing weight is painful and being obese is also painful but I had developed a tolerance for the misery of being obese, even though it was killing me.

But two and a half years after starting my healthy lifestyle journey, I owe all the praise, honour and glory to The Creator. He has given me the strength and the endurance to last as long as I have, and for the progress that I've made. Looking back at those years, there were many times when I just wanted to quit but He never allowed me to. He had many opportunities to judge me and give up on me but He was committed to holding my hand, even when I complained that my knees hurt, I was tired, or when I ate or did something that I wasn't supposed to.

I am thankful for His mercy and kindness. His meekness met me at my lowest and stayed with me ever since. I of all people should know how integral it is to have that love and support, and make it a priority to show grace to others, rather than the guilt trip I loved sending people on. I used my tongue like a sniper to damage people; they didn't see where it was coming from. I shouldn't have pushed people down to feel better about myself.

Derek Hough said it accurately in his speech about bullying, "You can be a beautiful skyscraper or you can tear down all the buildings around you to make yourself feel big, even though you're not." He also said, "Let's create. Let's not destroy."

1st Corinthians 13: 4-5 NKJV

*"Love suffers long and is kind; love does not envy;
love does not parade itself, is not puffed up;
Does not behave rudely, does not seek its own,
is not provoked, thinks no evil."*

Chapter XI

DELAYED, NOT DENIED

Thursday 23 April, 2015

Father, I'm writing this with a heavy heart, because if there was ever a time my faith was being tested, it's now. You have said that even if we have faith as small as a mustard seed, we can say, "Be removed, mountain" and it shall be removed, because nothing is impossible with you. That's exactly the amount of faith that I have left. It's as small as a mustard seed and I need your help to write this because the wound is fresh. I don't have time to clean things up, but I'm going to write it anyway.

I met a guy through a dating website. It's a highly reputable site and I've been on and off it for the past five years with no luck, but exactly eight days ago that all changed. It was an ordinary day. I woke up, went to the market with my grandpa and my mother, and when we got back, I checked my emails and saw that I had a flirt. Now I've been on that site for so long that I've seen almost all the profiles, so when I saw the name it was familiar. I took a deep breath, and went to the site to read his profile. It was the first profile that I read in a long time where the person actually communicated exactly what he was looking for. It was very detailed and I was intrigued but skeptical. I thought that's fine, I just read the profile so it was natural to feel this way. There was an option to click yes, I'm interested and I really wanted to but before I did, I prayed. I asked the Father to let this guy be the last guy I have to say yes, I'm interested to. I was so tired and fed up of putting myself out there, but worse than that, anytime it didn't work out, I felt like I was the problem. But after my prayer, I decided to go for it so I clicked and waited.

Imagine the joy I felt, reading his profile and seeing some of the things that I had on my wish list. I am 30 years old and only ever had one boyfriend who I met when I was 21 years of age. That relationship lasted for 5 years so you do the math. My biological clock is ticking now and I want companionship. Back to the guy. I've never checked my mail so many times in one day. That night I must have gotten 3 hours of sleep; I read his profile over so many times. Finally, around 4 a.m. the next morning I got a message from him, so I was now able to communicate with him. He introduced himself, complimented me on my smile, and I blushed like crazy. I complimented him on his communication skills because that's a plus in my book.

We sent messages to each other on the site but we decided to use another social media site, which made for easier and faster communication. That was day three after meeting.

I was still re-reading his profile because I wanted something to develop between us. I tried my hardest to dismiss and justify the parts of his profile that were not sitting well with me. When we connected on social media, the very first thing I asked was what stood out about my profile and he responded, "Noooo, you're really testing me here." Then he mustered, "You look really innocent and sweet… Oh what the hell, your brown eyes and your smile doesn't hurt either." I replied, "Oh okay," and he said, "Oh no, I see that was a bad answer." I told him that there wasn't a bad or good answer, I just wanted to know what stood out to him.

I was so happy to be chatting with him that I quickly stifled and ignored my instincts, just to keep the conversations going. When he told me what stood out to him, I thought, out of everything that I wrote about myself, that's what stood out to you? I felt the uneasiness increasing but I wanted him to be "the one" so badly. I tried to change where that apprehension was coming from I didn't want to accept that it was my spirit of discernment doing its job. I wanted it to be the enemy trying to keep me from my fairy-tale ending.

I managed to shut my instincts up for a while but that night I couldn't sleep, thinking about him. So I prayed but it was one of those careful prayers. You know, like when you really want something and deep down you know you're not supposed to have it, but you're asking anyway and eating up your words. Your volume lowers and the speed of your speech accelerates, hoping that the person you're asking would miss some key words. And then you convince yourself that you heard yes.

My prayer was similar, but I couldn't shake my uneasy feeling. We continued chatting and about two days later, I really couldn't fight it any longer. I had to give in and start praying the way I knew I should have in the beginning. But I was so scared, and that's exactly how I started my prayer. "Father I'm scared to ask you because I have a feeling the answer is no. I know I said that I don't want just a boyfriend, I want a husband, and I'm willing to wait on who you send but it's hard waiting on you. However, in spite of my fear, please reveal unto me, is it yay or nay?"

To my great surprise, that evening we chatted more than we ever did during the past 5 days, and he cleared up some of my concerns. Everything was going well. He sent me two voice messages, and his voice sounded like trumpets from heaven. As we say in Trinidad, ah GT (Get Through). I felt comfortable enough to the point where I gave myself a pep talk to come out of my comfort zone and asked if it would be okay for me to call him that night and he agreed.

I'm no athlete, but let me tell you, inside I was an Olympian — back handspring, cart wheels, you name it. At 9 p.m., I sent a message asking if it was a good time to call. He didn't reply until about an hour later to inform me that he was a bit busy tying up some work with his accountant. He apologized and said he would call me the next day. I told him to take care of his responsibilities and I would talk to him tomorrow, and we said goodnight to each other.

That night I prayed so hard, and the next day I prayed even more intensely. Around 3:30 p.m. that afternoon, I started to feel a burning sensation in my stomach. I walked up the stairs, into my bedroom and had this urge to read a book that I've been trying to read since December of last year. We're in April now and I haven't looked at that book for about three weeks. Anyway, I picked it up and I read for almost two hours. I've never spent so much time reading anything before.

I can't remember if I mentioned before but I do not like to read, which makes it even more ridiculous that I'm writing a book. Oddly enough, I just couldn't stop reading this book. I felt my body getting cold; everything I read was confirmation of the unrest I felt, but chose to ignore for the past week. My mother was sitting in the room with me so I had to take some really deep breaths to hold back the tears, because I was hurting like hell. Even though I pretty much knew the answer from the beginning, it didn't take anything away from the disappointment.

By the time I finally put the book down, I knew the answer. He was not the man for me, but I was still wishing that the confirmation wasn't coming from The Father, but rather Satan trying to fight me for what was rightfully mine (I was desperate). So I was still waiting and hoping for his call.

I was going to take a shower but just as intensely as the urge to read the book, I felt the urge to ride my stationary bike. I thought it was strange because what I really wanted to do was crawl into my bed and cry. Besides, that bike had been my clothes rack for the past few months, but I lost that debate so I jumped on it and started to ride feverishly, still wrestling with my answer.

I decided that I also needed to listen to some really up-tempo music to drown out the thoughts in my head, so I put on my head set and went to YouTube from my phone. How convenient that the very first video that was recommended was 'Say No To The Flesh' by Joel Osteen. There was a magnet pulling me to listen to it so I pressed play. The video was 29 minutes long and I felt like he prepared it just for me. The only thing he didn't do was call my name.

I stopped riding as soon as he stopped preaching; I was in shock and very disappointed. Earlier that day I spoke to my mother about everything that was happening so she knew that I was seeking some answers. She walked into my room at the exact time that I stopped riding and I said, "The answer is No." She paused and looked at me because she knew how I felt. She asked me how I knew and I replied with, "How I always know."

Then and there I prayed again. "Father it's painful enough that the answer is no so please don't let him ever call me or even message me ever again. I can't deal with the reminder of what I thought could have been. And if everything that happened wasn't confirmation enough, the fact that he hasn't even attempted to contact me, and the fact that he left the site, is more than enough proof."

By that time, I was desperate. If you remember, earlier I wrote that my two greatest desires were to be a wife and a mother. It's all I ever dream of. I would be perfectly contented just honouring those two roles, but it hasn't happened yet, which has me feeling angry and frustrated. And I'm not angry with the man because he didn't do anything wrong. He just wasn't the man for me, but that's what's so frustrating. I keep meeting men that are not mine and that process is a daunting one.

I don't know, it just seems as though the more effort I make to do the things the master commanded me to do, the less favourable my rewards are; and it's not only in my head because my current reality holds the proof. It's frustrating to see the people that I grew up with, some of them younger, married with children. People used to laugh at me for always talking about wanting a family while everyone else was fully exploring their teenage years and dreaming about their careers. Now I'm 30, and single with no children. As unconventional as it may sound in this modern society, it's my simple dream and what I equate with peace, joy and happiness. I feel like I will impact this world for good by being the best wife and mother that the grace of The Father allows me to be, by sacrificially serving them my love, time and support so that they could reach their fullest potentials.

There are two perspectives in this situation and I know which one I should take, but I have to ask, does faith really work? What a question to ask, but that's what is floating around in my head right now. When I hear some people's testimonies, I think that I should enjoy my life more. Live a rebellious lifestyle until I was well and ready to come back, and ask for forgiveness and get my blessings. I understand how foolish that sounds but that's where my mind takes me sometimes. I've read the story of the prodigal son many times before and naturally, the focus is on his character because he is the main man. But honestly, the more time I spend sacrificially trying to serve The Master, the more I relate to the prodigal brother. And again, I'm not saying that I'm a saint because you read for yourself that I'm not, I just wish that in spite of all the wrong I've done, my sentence of nothingness could be reduced.

I am grappling with jealousy and anger. Whenever I'm going through any type of disappointment or heartbreak, my head automatically organizes people's lives into "happy" thumbnails. Showing their engagement rings, or some who are already happily married, with their seemingly perfect family portraits.

And I'm still Ms. Shemelia Henry. No boyfriend, no children, not even a dog, well except for the dog that appeared outside my gate about three weeks ago. I named him Miguel, but bottom line is, he's still not my dog.

Anyway, the point here is that I feel like I'm the only person dealing with this frustration. It feels like one big conspiracy. Just when I'm struggling to make it through the day, a friend would call just as happy as she can be, to announce that she's getting married. Or, I'll be casually browsing through social media to see another friend poetically pouring her soul into a post about how eternally grateful she is to have a new life growing inside of her. Then, another friend would post about 10,000 pictures of herself and the new boyfriend with, "I'm so thankful that I met you, love you babes, smiley face! #myking #mybae"

It's beyond my comprehension why I'm expected to be happy for them. Really, why? When we both prayed for the same thing and her prayer was answered while mine apparently floated away into the abyss. I have a good reason to feel angry. Why shouldn't I feel sorry for myself? All I'm asking for is something that The Father himself agrees with, "It is not good that man should be alone." And that verse isn't even far in the Bible, it's right there in Genesis 2:18 NKJV!

Monday 27 April, 2015. 11:09 a.m.

**Father, please help me; teach me not to covet.
Remove the spirit of jealousy from me;
give me patience with this process.**

It's been four days since I last wrote anything, and in case you were wondering, the guy still hasn't contacted me. Anyway, I feel so deflated.

So many of the same questions are running through my mind, Why me? What am I doing wrong? And the most important one, what is this situation here to teach me? I'll keep it real, that was the very last question I asked myself because nobody wants to be taught a lesson while dealing with disappointment and hurt.

I got some answers. It's not that I didn't know them already, but sometimes the answers are just too hard to accept. The first one is that timing is everything. He is in control; He will deliver, but you must have a good attitude while you wait. There is no doubt that I don't like those answers, but the bottom line is that I'm not in control. I tried, and I failed.

I'm currently off the dating site again and I'm praying for the strength to stay off for good this time. I'm not supposed to be hunting down a husband. My husband would be looking for me and he'll know he found me when he sees me. I can't wait for that great day when our Father masterfully orchestrates our divine meeting. Our purpose would align; there would be no doubt in our minds and for everything else, the Father would provide peace and grace.

I'm a novice when it comes to relationships but I'm going to give my opinion anyway. I made a list of what I want in a husband and who I want to be as a wife, but I realized that while it's good to have a vision, don't make it so structured and detailed that you miss what The Father has planned. I'm learning that the hard way.

Also, to all of my single ladies who want to be married, let's use this time wisely to figure out who we really are. We are nurturers and planners by nature but I'll speak more for myself. It's hard for me to distinguish how to show that I care without placing myself on the back burner. I'm always in fix it mode; I become consumed with trying to make everything right for others that they forget that I also need attending to, so I end up feeling empty.

So let's spend as much time as we can, praying and meditating on the scripture so that we would be made whole and loved, and know our worth. I think that being a wife is the true essence of what it means to be a woman, but we don't become wives just because we get married; the title wouldn't magically change us. There is so much more to it. Proverbs 31 is my favourite scripture on how to be a virtuous woman and I read it all the time. Go figure — that was my user name on the dating site, "proverbs31woman."

Men, do not give up your power. By nature, you are hunters but you must have that confidence in yourself and the only way to find that is to seek The Master for your instructions. If you do, He would direct your steps; He will send you to the right woman. Your job is a mighty one; in singleness, study what it takes to be the spiritual leader of a home. Figure out what it is you truly need in a wife from her character, not her physical appearance. Yes, I know that looks hold some level of importance but not very much, and once you figure out what you need, trust The Father to show you your Eve.

Proverbs 18: 22 NKJV

"He who finds a wife finds a good thing,
and obtains favour from YAHWEH!"

Yahweh is hearing us but his delay is not denial. We just have to wait on his timing. Sure, we can prematurely make things happen but we'll only be doing ourselves an injustice. It may feel like it's taking an eternity, but we deserve to be appreciated, not just tolerated.

Let us praise Yahweh in the midst of our pain. Praising The Creator in spite of our pain will accelerate our blessing because that requires faith.

Mark 11: 24 NKJV

"Therefore I say to you, whatever things you ask,
when you pray, believe that you receive them,
and you will have them."

Psalms 27:13-14 NKJV

"I would have lost heart, unless I had believed
that I would see the goodness of Yahweh in the land of the living.
Wait on Yahweh; be of good courage,
and he shall strengthen your heart; wait, I say, on Yahweh."

Chapter XII
DECEPTION

For many years, I wondered if I missed the memo, that somehow the manual for life eluded me. Why couldn't I escape this hell of nothingness, this barren place that I've called home for most of my life? Why couldn't I do something right?

Because of my desperate need to be "enough" and in perfect standing with Yahweh, I became a people pleaser; my life was performance driven. And of course, after a great performance, I expected to be rewarded favourably. I felt that if I was more polite and I gave more smiles and good cheers, the faster my blessings would come.

Every day, I woke up with an agenda on how I was going to get Yahweh to bless me. As overwhelming as it was, I tried my best to keep inventory of every thought, every word and every deed in my everyday life. I placed immense pressure on myself to be perfect, even though perfection is unattainable.

My teen and early adult years were as bland and predictable as you could imagine. I never pushed the boundaries, I didn't explore, and I didn't ask questions. All I had was plan A, which was to get married and have children. That's it, no backup plan. I didn't want life to be angry at me so I settled for walking in the middle of the lane, where I thought would be safer. My belief at the time was, if I don't push the boundaries and just did what I thought was the right thing all the time, I would gain points.

Everything was for points. Whether it was giving a compliment or feeling a sense of pride when people I knew made a mistake or failed at something. Their mistakes made me feel like I was better than they were and I believed that Yahweh would realize that and give me the blessings that I deserved. My logic was the more points I got, the quicker it would take me out of the realm of uncertainty that I was suffocating in. I relied heavily on my system but there was a problem. It was not working out the way I thought it would at all, because I made mistakes of my own. But I was so committed to my agenda of collecting points that I held on to my notion that the right things would outweigh my mistakes. So I smiled, I was polite, and I did basically anything I thought was worthy of points.

I've heard so many wonderful things about how Yahweh feels about us. That we're all his masterpieces, and we're all uniquely made. He knows us by name, but receiving that is hard when you're under attack. I felt like there was no bandage big enough for my wounds; they spread so far and deep, and the pain was just unbearable. I searched for people who had the same symptoms as me, and took their advice and tried to apply it to my situation, but it didn't take long to realize that not because two people have the same symptoms means that they have the same problem.

I listened to hundreds of testimonies. Every day I sat with my laptop just absorbing peoples' testimonies of healing broken bondages, overcoming trauma, and lots more, which got my hopes up. So all I thought I had to do was replicate what they had done. Some of it required that I speak to Yahweh, that I challenge Him to do the things that He promised to do. So I'd shout out, "Are you real?" "If you're really who you say you are, then do something!" Some people said that's what they did when they were at their lowest and it worked for them, but not for me. This made me furious at Yahweh. On a few occasions I said, "If you don't do something soon, I'm joining the next team." I was going to stop having faith. I didn't mean it but I was desperate. I thought if I threatened Him, He would at least turn His face to me. But none of my strategies worked, and unfortunately it just reaffirmed all the lies that I believed from the enemy.

I wondered how there could be a plan of restoration for everyone else but me, especially when I was trying so hard. I came up with a plan to compartmentalize my problems to keep from becoming overwhelmed. The plan was to tackle my physical appearance first and when I got "slim and beautiful," my attitude would naturally become more positive, and everything else would fall into place.

Needless to say, that didn't work, not even for a week. I ate next to nothing for two days and when I weighed myself, I didn't even lose 1 pound. I was devastated. My head was in chaos; I felt angry, disappointed, and sad. I didn't really pray much at that time because I didn't feel like my prayers were being heard anyway. I read the bible but it felt like a chore that I had to get out of

But as angry and frustrated as I was, there was something inside me that wouldn't allow me to give up, even though I really wanted too.

I felt like I wasn't good enough for this world and I certainly wasn't good enough for Yahweh. One Sunday morning, my mother went to the market and I stood by the back door, looking at the mountains and praying, tears streaming down my face. My hands were up in defeat as I asked Yahweh to please take me out of this pain, even if that meant me dying. I just wanted out. But the second the words left my mouth, an image of my mother in anguish filled my mind. It was graphic enough that I apologized out loud. To be honest, I wasn't really apologizing to Him, I was only considering how my mother would feel.

My mother was the only person that I cared about devastating; even though I felt like it wouldn't matter if I lived or died. I wasn't making any contribution or positive impact to the lives of others. I was just taking up valuable space by being alive. No one knew how expensive my smile was during those times. People expected me to greet them with a smile because that's what I do, but the moment I didn't give them what they expected, they instantly came to the conclusion that I was angry. I wanted so badly to ask, "Am I not allowed to express other emotions? How is it that the moment I'm not passing out smiles and laughter, I'm angry?" I've been asked so many times why I'm angry. Not out of concern, but because I wasn't wearing the painted on smile that I usually have. In a way, I don't blame them because I was the one who programmed the robot that I'd become and I had to deal with it. I wish that I'd been bold enough to say that my smile was very expensive, and if you knew how expensive, then maybe you'd find value in it rather than always expecting it; not taking me for granted in the way that you'd expect to find sand at the beach.

My life was a total mess and it was not detectable, not even to the people closest to me. I desperately needed help but I was too scared and ashamed to ask for it. I prayed that somebody would just look at me, know that something was wrong, and demand that the real me stand up. That he or she would commit to investing however long a time that was required for me to heal.

That's another deception of the enemy — to make us believe that we're entitled to people forsaking their duties and their lives to pursue our problems. And when they don't, he turns around and convinces us that all we have and can depend on is ourselves, because how could the all loving Father allow us to suffer like this?

Before we know it, we become devoted to that belief but when Yahweh chooses you He'll pursue you, and that's exactly what He has been doing in my life. It's hard to see past our mistakes, failures and hardships when the concepts of victory and hope seem dead. But when Yahweh starts something, even when it appears that He has lost His way, He hasn't. I remember looking at a family vlog on YouTube where they went into a corn maze and were having so much fun, walking through the cleared out paths. Once in a while, they got lost and reached so many dead ends but that didn't stop them. In fact, they were laughing hysterically and I found myself laughing along with them. Then it dawned on me — my life is like a corn maze!

If only I could apply the concept of a corn maze to my life, I thought. I assumed the purpose of the activity was for mental stimulation and entertainment. Whether that's the case or not, one thing's for certain — it's not meant to frustrate you. Yes, life is challenging and I'm going to reach some dead ends. But rather than setting up camp, it should force me to stop and recalibrate, and continue on my journey. It's all about the experiences that I go through in the maze of life that would mould, shape, extract, and deposit all that I need to become the person that Yahweh envisioned. And because of all of that, I'll never be the same person that I was when I first entered this maze; I'll be much stronger.

What a revelation. Rather than trying to use my strength and finite ability to overcome my issues, why not truly surrender all to Him and ask my infinite Heavenly Father to be my compass? I'll lose a few things in the maze but I know I'm insured with Him. It's such a relief to understand that I don't have to make things happen for myself.

I'm not saying that I should toss discipline, morals or self-awareness to the wind, or that I should just "do me" and trust that all the facets of grace will incubate me. It may not, and it's all because of that double-edged sword called knowledge. Once you've been enlightened, it's done. You can't call forth selective amnesia so that you can continue doing what you used to, and be expecting favourable rewards.

If you're like me, even after your mind has started the healing process, you're not going to instantly let go of the vice grip you had on your life. The more you immerse yourself in the presence of Yahweh, the easier it would become to trust and fall into His hands. Don't be like me and make a strict plan for your life, and shut it down so tight that you don't leave room for Yahweh to come in, navigate, and authenticate it.

Genesis 3: 8-11 NKJV

*"And they heard the sound of Yahweh walking in the garden
in the cool of the day, and Adam and his wife hid themselves
from the presence of Yahweh among the trees of the garden.
Then Yahweh called to Adam, and said to him, "Where are you?"
So he said, 'I heard Your voice in the garden,
and I was afraid because I was naked; and I hid myself.'
And He said, who told you that you were naked?"*

We always have two voices speaking to us and our life is a direct reflection of which one we yield our ears to. The enemy's job is to deceive us at all costs. He takes pleasure in making us feel ashamed for all the wrong that we've done. And because we feel like our sins were too grave to be forgiven, we try to block them out of our heads. The dangerous thing with that is every time we don't repent, the more desensitized we become — that's what the enemy is counting on. But, we have a Heavenly Father who loves us so much that He gave His only begotten son to die for our sins. Our debt has already been paid. Everything that is right and good is of Yahweh. He cannot do anything bad. He will never lead us into temptation so let us not hide ourselves like Adam and Eve did. Yahweh is the only one who can heal us, without judgment and without guilt.

St John 3:16-18 NKJV

*"For Yahweh so loved the world, that He gave
His only begotten son, that whoever believes in Him
should not perish, but have everlasting life.*

*For Yahweh did not send His Son into the world
to condemn the world; but that the world*

through Him might be saved.
He who believes in Him is not condemned;
but he who does not believe is condemned already,
because he has not believed in the name
of the only begotten Son of Yahweh."

Romans 5:8 NKJV

"But Yahweh demonstrates His own love toward us,
in that while we were still sinners, Yahsuah died for us."

Chapter XIII

LEGION

Luke 8:26-30 NKJV

*"Then they sailed to the country of the Gadarenes,
which is opposite Galilee.
And when He stepped out on the land,
there met Him a certain man
from the city who had demons for a long time.
And he wore no clothes, nor did he live in a house but in the tombs.
When he saw Yahsuah, he cried out, fell down before Him,
and with a loud voice said, 'What have I to do with You, Yahsuah,
Son of The Most High Yahweh? I beg You, do not torment me!'
For He had commanded the unclean spirit to come out of the man.
For it had often seized him, and he was kept under guard,
bound with chains and shackles;, and he broke the bands,
and was driven by the demon into the wilderness.
Yahsuah asked him, saying, 'What is your name?'
And he said, 'Legion,' because many demons had entered him."*

You should read the entire story! I've read it a few times before, but like so many of the other bible stories I've read, they all seemed theatrical to me. For the greater part of my life thus far, it has been very difficult to grasp the significance and power of the words in the bible. That is, until life dealt with me, served me a paradigm shift like no other, and opened my eyes to how alive the scriptures are.

I don't view the bible now as some cosmic experience documented simply for my entertainment, but rather as an exclusive overview of the lives of actual people who lived and died before me. Through divine inspiration, they have left me words of encouragement, instructions, and the answers to every question that I would ever have.

The word legion means a vast number of people or things. It's both shocking and unsettling how much I relate to the man in that story, who had a legion of demonic spirits dwelling inside of him. So too, my mind was being controlled by a legion of demonic spirits. As unsettling as it is, it now makes sense why my mind was being tossed around like a Frisbee. I kept latching on to one self-inflicting deadly emotion to the next. I've hurt people from time to time but the real damage happened in my own life.

Fear, anger, doubt, depression, insecurity, pride, insufficiency, self-hatred, anxiety — just to name a few, are some of the spirits that took turns possessing my mind.

As a result, I spent my life volunteering to be defeated, in one way or the other, and I didn't even know it. I thought that was just my life, that's the way it was meant to be. It's difficult to explain but it felt like my mind was in this constant tennis match between truth and lies. I was in so much conflict, I heard voices telling me that the truth were lies and the lies were truth. And because my mind was already a cohort of the enemy, I believed the lies and thought it was the truth.

Despite all the chaos in my head, there was always something inside me that kept me going, even when I couldn't see a way out. It kept me sane when I thought I was losing my mind. It prompted me to read the bible even though I didn't understand what I was reading. It was frustrating, but I kept reading anyway. My grandpa always told me to read the bible if even I don't understand it right away. "That's ok, just keep reading and The Father will reveal it to you at the right time," he said and that's exactly what The Father did for me with that particular scripture. I know the thoughts that I have and the way those thoughts make me feel, but I never would have considered that those dark thoughts could be spirits, fighting me for my head. What a relief to know that I'm not as messed up as I thought I was. I believed for so many years that it was me; that's just the way I was made, that obscurity was my destiny.

As long as I settled with the bondages and strongholds in my life, I was good with the enemy. He didn't need to fight me if he got me. It was entertainment enough watching me fight myself and self-destruct. It exhausted me; I didn't know that I was fighting an army. All I knew was that I felt disadvantaged and now I see why I felt that way. My opponent wasn't fair — he walked in with his whole dysfunctional family to fight me and for every punch I fired and missed, he and his team attacked more aggressively.

I was a hardcore pity partier, but after a few days I'd sober up from that drunken state. After allowing the enemy to intoxicate me with his lies, I'd realize what I was doing wrong and try to soothe myself. But I'm really low on patience so when I pray and I don't see anything happening, I take matters into my own hands — which makes everything a hundred times worse. Trust and believe me — it ain't easy.

You see, when my wounds finally start to heal and get a scab, sometimes I have to pick off the scab to allow new flesh to grow back. Although it's more painful than getting the actual wound in the first place, I'd much rather do the picking myself — that way I'd be able to gauge the pain and regulate the process. When Yahweh does it, I never know when or how he is going to do it, and that uncertainty scares me so much. But after going through so much, I've decided that I'd rather feel my way through uncertainty than walk off a cliff with my eyes wide open, simply because it's familiar. Been there, done that.

I am so thankful for the beacon of light that The Father hid inside of me, where nothing or no one was ever granted access. The Holy Spirit alone dwells there, and the fact that I could even write this is evidence that I haven't been forsaken. He, in spite of all the lies that I held on to, still equipped me with some tenacity and authority to push through every degrading and intimidating thought, and listen to His truth. I'm not going to lie, His truth felt minuscule compared to the amount of lies I already believed about myself. But I held on because only the Father could cause someone who felt so hopeless to feel even the tiniest bit of hope.

You created me Father; you hold the blueprint for my life.

Chapter XIV
IDENTITY

The battle isn't on the outside of me, it's on the inside.
And the sooner I stop being so reactionary,
the more peace I'd have in my life.

If no one else was impacted by that, I hope and pray that I am. I pray that those words would become so ingrained that I can be like the still, deep waters undisturbed by the surface waves; and like the palm tree whose roots become stronger, after the storms came.

I am at a point in my journey where I have to get rid of some of the emotions that I've been hoarding for most of my life. Feelings of Hurt, Resentment, Abandonment, Anger, Jealousy, Confusion, and Brokenness.

I realize that I was looking to so many different things and people in my life to find my identity, but I never found it. I have a few ideas as to why I wasn't finding it: (1) I didn't know what I was looking for exactly; therefore how could I have known if I found it? (2) I was looking in all the wrong places to begin with.

Monday 22 June, 2015

Identity – the distinguishing character or personality of an individual. Merriam-Webster Dictionary

The word Identity never really crossed my mind until yesterday when I heard someone talking about it. The things he said made so much sense and got my attention because the past two weeks have been really frustrating. It all started when my stepmother called to invite my mother and I to my dad's surprise Father's Day lunch. At first, I was fine with it and so was my mother but as the hours went by, my anger started to build because I hadn't spoken to my dad since my birthday on January 16th.

That makes it about 5 months since I spoke to my dad. To be fair, he shouldn't have to stand all the blame. I could have called as well, but during that time I was too busy keeping record of how long he could go without hearing my voice.

In my head, there's only one logical explanation for why he wasn't trying to contact me. He has all he needs in my four other siblings; after all, I haven't done a single thing to make him proud enough to want to love me.

I mentioned earlier that the way I felt I could gain love from people was by going out of my way to make them happy, whether that meant giving them something or giving my time, anything for them to recognize that I was a good person.

At age 30, I find myself feeling like a little girl, longing for love and acceptance from her dad.

It's not always easy, practicing what you preach. I know that in this life, I have to run my own race but every now and then I drift into other people's lanes, and with the help of the pathological liar within, I start comparing myself with them. I've always been jealous of my siblings and truth is, I don't really know them. Every time we meet, it feels like the first time to me. It's hard to move past that point to form any kind of relationship with them because I'm always so self-conscious and angry with them. I'm jealous because I'm the only one who has never spent a single night under the same roof with our father, and he never came to any of my schools. What hurts the most is hearing them call him daddy. It's second nature for them but for me, it's the most awkward feeling. I feel like such an imposter every time so I rarely ever call him anything at all, I usually just start speaking.

Anyway, let me rewind to just a few days before the lunch on Father's Day. I decided that I wouldn't attend and I justified it by believing he wouldn't miss me anyway. So the day before, I called my stepmother and lied about why I couldn't make it. I solidified it by telling her that my mother had to work that day anyway, so that worked itself out perfectly.

> "When you're angry your mind is like a see-saw,
> your Emotions are high and your Reasoning is low."
>
> **Deborah Pegues**

That night I was so angry with my father and myself. Truth is, I really wanted to go. I wanted to be like everyone else, celebrating their father. But I couldn't because I felt like he robbed me of the chance of doing so. Later that night I made up my mind that I was done.

I had enough of secretly hoping that my father would call me one day and apologize, and explain why he wasn't more involved in my life. As the tears flowed down my face, I started to pray. I asked The Heavenly Father to be my father, to help me to be okay without an earthly father. I left my heart open for so long, waiting for my earthly father to come in and take his place, but he passed on every opportunity.

On Father's Day, I called him three times out of formality but I didn't get him. He called back once but I missed the call, which I was okay with, and we finally spoke the next morning. I felt relieved when that task was over with.

Later on, I listened to a man talking about marriage on You Tube and meeting your spouse's needs. He spoke about some needs that no other person can meet, and one of them was the need for "Identity." It piqued my interest but I wrestled with the possibility that I was still searching for my identity. I didn't want to believe that but the more he explained it, the more I identified with what he said.

Every time I hit a low point in my life there were always two questions that I'd ask myself: "Why was I born?" and "What's my purpose?" But I didn't realize that my search kept coming up empty because I was asking the wrong questions, which undoubtedly predetermined the wrong answers.

Since it is the sole purpose of the enemy to distort the truth and keep me disoriented, I made his job a lot easier by allowing my pain and despair to overpower the truth. Truth is, I was born for a reason —The Heavenly Father has a plan for me and He will fulfil it.

All that talk about identity really gave me something to think about so I decided to pray and fast that whole week from six to six. I needed answers; the emotions I felt towards my father were so strong. I was very angry and I could feel it turning into rage; it was consuming me so I needed to take drastic measures.

When I started the fast, I intended to be free of those bondages. I just wanted peace of mind, but somewhere along the way, I started believing that I was a victim. Before I knew it, I found myself praying that my father would start feeling guilty for not being there for me, which worked for a while, so imagine my surprise when I started to feel convicted. The enemy is so tricky — he had me contradicting myself.

Tuesday 23 June, 2015. 5:37 p.m.

Today I listened to Touré Roberts preach one of his sermons, "You Will Lack Nothing." Ironically, it was his Father's Day message. The passage of scripture he read was

Psalms 27: 10 NKJV

"When my father and my mother forsake me,
Then Yahweh will take care of me."

He talked about perspective, walking in other people's shoes, and that we're all broken. I mean, he laid it on thick and what he said made perfect sense. I just wasn't ready to receive it because it didn't seem fair that he didn't say one thing to justify how I was feeling. I don't know how it happened, but by the time he was finished with his message, I got it. But, I still couldn't muster up the courage to forgive my father.

About half an hour after, grandpa called me on the phone. He cooked 'oil down' and he knows that I like it. The excitement in his voice was so awakening, you know, one of those "AHA" moments. I had to fight those tears back because he lives next door and I didn't want him to see me crying when I went over for the food. Just as I was coming off the phone, he told me to bring a bowl and laughed. He was so happy, knowing that he was going to make me happy. In that moment, I finally understood that I lacked nothing.

The word forsake in the above scripture means relinquish. The meaning of relinquish does not have to be bad — it's all about perspective. So for those of us whose parents have relinquished us, it doesn't feel good but Yahweh works everything out for our benefit in the end.

I am truly blessed to have my grandfather because he has been the male role model in my life. In my earlier years I was scared of him because he is a very stern man, but as I grew, I was enlightened daily by his wisdom. Our relationship today is one that I'm incredibly thankful for, more than I can describe. My nicknames for him are "grandpur" or "grandpa Ken." I can say for certain that I respect him more than anyone else on this earth, and he is also my friend.

"Delay is not denial Sheme. Hold on." That's what he always says to me. I'll admit that sometimes it's the hardest thing to believe, but his hope gives me hope. Thank you grandpa for being the spiritual leader of our home and for lovingly teaching us what you learnt — to have a personal relationship with the Master for ourselves. There is no doubt that because of my relationship with The Heavenly Father, I am able to forgive my earthly father. And because of the tender mercies that The Father has shown me, I'm able for the first time to even consider what my father's relationship was like with his dad. I have only seen my grandfather on my dad's side once, so I don't really know him. I know it wouldn't be easy, trying to undo all of the reasoning I made up in my head about my father, but I am willing to start.

Rather than measuring my father to others who are seemingly honouring their jobs as fathers, I'm now going to be thankful that he relinquished me early. Given the extent of my brokenness, my father may not have had the wisdom or the structure that was necessary to raise me, and it's possible that he may have further damaged me.

But Yahweh knew that (absolutely). My grandfather, being far from perfect, has been hurt many times in his life also, but he went to the Great Physician and was made whole again with a testimony to tell. Grandpa was the best person to nurse me. He had more tools to work with and knew exactly who to turn to for instructions on how to deal with me.

Like I said, anyone who knows him would testify that he's a very serious and stern man, but for some reason when it comes to me, he has so much patience and understanding. There is just something different; I can't quite put my finger on it, but it's there. His wisdom is unmistakable and I glean from it every day.

I love and thank my grandpa for being my earthly example of what it means to forgive, and how to trust in Yahweh for his finished work.

To my father, I wrote you a letter some years ago and I told you that I forgave you, but looking back on it, that was only me trying to manipulate you into validating me as your daughter. But today I truly forgive you. Not because it feels good or even because I want to, but because I have to. My Heavenly Father gave me my identity and if I want to continue to grow and become more like Him, I have to do what he commands me to do.

I want you to know that I love you, in spite of the fact that I grew up feeling like you didn't love me. And it's not that I automatically feel this overwhelming sense of love for you, because my feelings are subject to change at any given moment. It's because of a renewed and made up mind, that knows you were only a vessel that was used to bring me into this world. You didn't give me life, nor did you try to sustain it, but the one who give me life and can take it away said "Honour your father and your mother, that your days may be long upon the land." Exodus 20:12,

NKJV.

My father was only following instructions. I'm not trying to justify what he did but I'm simply choosing to attribute every experience in my life (both good and bad) to the perfectly imperfect purpose and destiny of my life. When I was a child, it was understandable for me to cast blame on my father for not taking care of his responsibilities. But the time has come where I have to take responsibility for my own life. My past — his actions, my hurt — does not and must not determine my future.

When all is said and done, I lack nothing.

I wrote about this to help those of us who survived that storm; to reflect on the shelter that our Heavenly Father provided us with while the winds were blowing. So we can go back and tell our stories to those who are presently in turmoil and show them that there is calm after the storm.

If I could say one thing to fathers, based on my experience: it doesn't matter what season of your life that your child was born. It's one of the biggest blessings and privileges that you would ever receive — to be entrusted with a life that is so precious to The Creator.

I know this is a bold prayer, but I pray that all men who have been favoured with a child would view it as such — a favour, being done for them by Yahweh. I pray that you would have the strength to ask for help and know that you do not have to be a perfect man to be a father. You don't need to have "everything" in place — use what you have. The good news is that your child would love you unconditionally. When the world criticizes you and puts you into a particular category, your child sees you as a hero.

So honour your position. It's okay to ask for help. Take the time you need to pray to our Heavenly Father about some of the things that you may have done in your life that you don't want to pass on to your child. Your sins do not have to fall on your child — you have that grace available to you. We all know that experience is the greatest teacher so use it in a positive way. Because you have learned from the consequences of certain actions in the past, you now get to utilize that knowledge in a way that would help shape your child in the way you would like. Go, do your part, and leave the rest to The Father. **"Train up a child in the way he should go, and when he is old, he will not depart from it."** Proverbs 22:6

NKJV.

Don't let your financial status stop you from being there for your child. I'm going on record to say that money is not important to children. They have no limits on their expectations, simply because they don't understand the value of money. What they understand and FEEL most of all is the value of your love, care, protection, and respect for them as "little" human beings. Respect them and they will respect you.

So money is not an excuse. Of course, it is your responsibility to provide for their needs but giving them things doesn't make much of an impact. Any person can give them things but that doesn't substitute for your presence. Things can be replaced, but not the time that you wasted. If you give a child a stone that you found in your back yard and you say that it's a special stone just for him, he will cherish that stone because it came from you. Children are blessed with this amazing ability to love unconditionally and a boundless imagination, so take advantage of that while you still can.

My little cousin 'drives' everything that he could get his hands on. He recently came into my room and drove my packs of chewing gum all over my bed and the walls. He used my perfume bottles as traffic lights, and I'm not going to lie — he drove me crazy, but his imagination cracks me up; I love him.

So, again fathers: you don't have to have it all together to do what's right. Truth is, you will never have it all together. You are a great influence in your children's lives so tell them that you love them, show them that you love them. Never stop praying for them, but most importantly, teach them to pray for themselves.

Chapter XV

Life Interrupted

Friday, 2 October, 2015. 2:03 p.m.

Hello Shemelia,

    I know that you're not doing too well right now. You only graduated secondary school with four passes, and because you felt unqualified, you never attempted to go back to school and do anything closely related to academics. Since you finished school, you've never really had a real job, so you feel worthless because you never contributed anything to society.

I know that you're scared out of your mind that someone would find out you're not who you pretend to be. I know that you feel very hollow, but as devastatingly lonely, degrading and painful as it feels, you'd much rather exist in your self-incarcerated world, rather than risk being exposed in the real world.

And yes, you don't meet the world's standard of beauty based on the fact that you're "morbidly obese." Your highest weight was 350 lbs. but I know that you've lost 105 lbs. and that's good. I understand that you're even more worried because you still have about 65 lbs. to lose and already you're breasts are sagging and you're scared about having loose skin. I know you feel like no matter what you do, you can't win.

Sunday 1 November, 2015

I vowed from the beginning of this book to be honest and transparent, so let me say that it's been three weeks since I've written anything. I just didn't have the zeal, my mind once again got the better of me. These past three weeks have been terrible.

The day I started writing that letter to myself, I meant to identify and shine a light on the things in my life that the enemy has been using to hold me hostage. I wanted to say to myself, "Yes, you are flawed but that doesn't define who you are. You are stronger than you think you are." However, my insecurities decided that if they were going to be trampled on, they weren't going down without a fight, so boy did they show up ready for battle.

I woke up around 11:30 p.m. that night to go pee. Before I could even open my eyes, the very first thought that came to my mind was, "Nobody cares about you and your so called book." That was just the beginning — before I knew it, I was bombarded with one criticizing thought after the other. "You don't even know what you're doing. You've never read a book from cover to cover in your entire life; what makes you believe that someone will take time out of their precious life to read your book? You've only written 73 pages so far, oh please what a joke. By the time it's edited it might be reduced to half that amount. You know yourself — you're not an author. You don't have anything to stand on academically, and no background in anything required to write a book. You have zero connections, why are you wasting your time?"

That, along with many other discouraging thoughts flooded my mind during the past few weeks, which brings me to this morning. I woke up at 3:14 a.m. and when I opened my eyes, my hand brushed up against my leg. It felt very dry and wrinkled and tears immediately filled my eyes. Again, the discouraging thoughts came. My life feels like it's just been going in circles, I can distinguish between lies and truth but I still allow the lies to pierce me.

For years, I thought my biggest problem was losing weight but it has become apparent that it isn't. I feel like I'm jumping from the pot directly into the fire. I feel stuck and scared. I want to continue losing the weight but my loose skin and sagging breasts make me feel like I'm between a rock and a hard place. I don't know what to do. I worry about how I would ever explain this to a man. This is a genuine and constant concern of mine.

The best way to describe how I feel right now is defeated. Maybe this could really be the end of this book, who knows. It's now 4:46 am and I'm sitting in the middle of my bed with my legs folded and my cover draped over me. I'm just a runaway train at this point. Conversations where I *felt like my voice wasn't being heard that I had with friends and family started replaying in my head. I don't even know why because they had nothing at all to do with my weight.*

This is what happens to me. It takes one thing to send me into a tailspin, and then there are a million thoughts flowing through my head. Wow, this time the enemy is really hitting me with his best shot, I think it might be lethal. I'm furious with myself and everyone else and I can't put my finger on exactly why, which makes it more frustrating.

Today's anger is not the main problem but yesterday's anger is. There is a new grace available to us each and every day, that allows us to deal with the issues at that time. But when we choose to walk away from our daily challenges, we end up like me — angry, judgmental, and with a distorted perception of people and life in general. I say this because most of the time I felt like everyone was out to get me. I didn't feel respected and I took offence pretty quickly. I knew that they were all lies but I bought into them every time.

Ecclesiastes 7:21-22 NKJV

*"Also do not take to heart everything people say,
lest you hear your servant cursing you.
For many times, also, your own heart has known
that even you have cursed others."*

Do yourself and your loved ones a favour — don't leave any space for the enemy to come in and lay his eggs on your sores.

Ephesians 4:26 NKJV

*"Be angry, and do not sin,
do not let the sun go down on your wrath."*

I allowed bitterness to grow in me and I was scared of my own anger. I feared that I was losing control of my sanity. I failed at trying to manage my mess by myself and I found myself awake in the wee hours of the morning when everyone else was peacefully resting, mad at the world, replaying and responding to conversations in my head.

Passive aggression is dishonesty, either to you or to the other person.

That wasn't good for my health but it was like that for so long. I was really frustrated and lost with those obstacles. I felt like it would finish me. I didn't have the strength that I started with, there was no fight left.

I wondered sometimes, "Did I hear correctly? Are my steps really ordered by Yahweh? Are his plans for my life for real?" I mean, this invasion by the enemy's camp was so forceful.

Back then, my past victories were my faintest memories, because I was bruised and bloody with dirt under my nails. I was tired, but I have to confess, every time I was thrown into the lion's den, I made it out alive, by no strength of my own. The trauma was so vivid, but I had to trust in Yah.

So about that letter to myself —facts are facts but your perspective is what truly matters. Know that as long as you are living you will have obstacles in your way, but you can do all things through Yahweh who strengthens you (Philippians 4:13, NKJV). So it's up to you; which are you going to focus on: the world's facts or Yahweh's Truth for you? I pray you focus on the latter. You may feel like you will never accomplish your dreams because they're ridiculous for "someone like you" but hang in there. You can't give up; you have lives to impact and way too much love to let it go to waste. So live selflessly and totally dependent on Yahweh, even in the most difficult situations. Don't accept defeat, don't preserve the temporary. The darkest hour of the night is just before dawn. My grandpa says that to me all the time.

May you be enlightened about your significance on this earth. May you be heavily armoured to help and inspire others. I pray that from here onwards, you'll humbly choose love as your shield, comforter and currency. May there be no room left for you to keep inventory of those who offended you.

Chapter XVI
INTROSPECTION

This past week has been challenging, both mentally and emotionally. I've been in yet another battle with the enemy. At first, I was completely unaware of what was happening but around the third day, I realized that something wasn't right. Even then, I couldn't figure out what was actually wrong with me. All I know is that I couldn't maintain my peace.

It was like a container that you're pouring water into, but there's a leak somewhere and you can't locate it. It doesn't matter how much water you pour, it's never full.

I am going to do my best to explain how I felt but to be honest, I'm still confused. This past week I experienced every emotion that there is to experience. The one thing that I did notice was the pattern. Every day was the same sequence. Every morning I woke up feeling like the weight of the world was on my shoulders, but after my morning prayer, I'd feel refreshed and filled with optimism.

Then the simplest thing would happen and all of my optimism would go away. Anxiety would take its place, which would then invite fear, and self-pity, which inevitably led to me crying and feeling depressed, angry, alone and confused. And just when I'd start to feel like I couldn't stand any longer, the oddest thing would happen. A sense of calm would drape over me, and for the rest of the day I'd be perfectly fine — until the next morning when the whole cycle would start all over again.

After what felt like the most exhausting week of my life, having to ride this emotional roller coaster, I forced myself to take a time out so I could take an introspective look at things, and I think I found one of the reasons why I've been feeling so empty lately. I've lost my hopefulness, my zeal and my desire to dream. The enemy cleverly found a way to remove the gloss from all that I've been praying for. After many years of trying to convince me that I wasn't worthy to receive what I was praying for, he switched gears; he is now attacking me from a different angle. Now he's trying to get me to relinquish my strength and accept defeat. I found myself contented in what should only be my transition phase.

I must admit, at first he got me. Everything is easier when I don't have any expectations which is what the enemy was capitalizing on. He is very thorough and always has a backup plan. He must have thought that since he couldn't get me to stop hoping and believing for what I desire, why not make what I'm hoping for seem less desirable? And that he did.

I am finally realizing that everything has a price, and some sacrifices are greater than others are. I saw a TV ad about a new price-matching feature. The store claimed that if you could show that the price for a particular item is cheaper at another store, they'd drop their price to match. I thought that if only I had that feature in my life, things would definitely be easier. But I don't have that luxury, the process cost what it cost. Sometimes, from where I'm standing, it seems like others pay less but the price of true victory is sacrificial for all of us.

Matthew 5:45 NKJV

"That you may be sons of your Father in heaven, for He makes His sun rise on the evil and on the good, and sends rain on the just and on the unjust."

Dreaming is good and without it, we'd be lost. However, there has to be intent, determination and action behind it to bring it to fruition. Fantasizing is probably one of the most natural things to do, but we rarely ever expect disappointments or consider the length of time it could possibly take to accomplish whatever it is that we're dreaming of. There's where the enemy gets us every time. When we leave those little cracks, he makes full use of them.

When we dream, we dream with the result in mind. We expect everything to work in our favour, and when reality doesn't reflect any improvements, it's easy to question ourselves and Yahweh.

Heavenly Father, I pray that the eyes of our understanding would be open to the plots of the enemy, but more importantly, your plans for our life.

It doesn't matter how accomplished, knowledgeable, or respected we are on any level. Whenever we get to the next level, we will always have to start from the bottom, which will make us wonder, is this really a blessing? Because it surely won't feel like much of one.

The enemy thinks he has us right where he wants us to make his move, but He that began the good work in us will see it through to the end. I have to keep telling myself that, even if I have to fake believe it. I have to be persistent.

Do you remember the room with the glass walls that I spoke about at the beginning of the book? Well, the difference now is that I'm outside of that room, but I'm still feeling all the emotions that I felt while I was in it and it's confusing because this is what I prayed for. I prayed for an opportunity to get out of that mentally incarcerated box. And now that I'm finally starting to figure out what I'm meant to be doing with my life, and I've mustered up some strength to accept the challenges along the path to my destiny, it appears like I have underestimated the cost. It's all very lonely and overwhelming. It's a scary feeling.

My biggest fear is failure, and I feel like I'm on the fast track to that. I envisioned something completely different from my current reality. I never thought that I would find myself with my nose pressed up against the glass wall, looking in, longing to go back into that room because everything there, though stifling, is familiar.

THE DEVIL IS A LIAR.
Father, release me from the fantasy of immediately finding where I fit on the next level. Give me the wisdom and the patience to know when to walk and when to stand still.

Teach me to be content with where I am in the process,
and to stop trying to overcompensate
for whom I haven't developed into yet.
Teach me humility to realize that it doesn't matter
how much I think I know, there will always be someone
who knows more than I do. In that case,
I pray for the divine mechanics of knowing
just when to shut up and listen.
Open my eyes to every blessing that is in my life,
especially those that don't seem like blessings —
all of the NOs, Shut Doors, Barrenness, and Barriers.
Shift my perception on disappointments.

Chapter XVIII
DEPRESSION, SUICIDE, HOPE

Monday 01 February, 2016.

Here I am, making another entry into this book. I thought that I was finished three months ago; I made contact with a publisher and was scheduled to start the publishing process, but for some unexplainable reason I just wasn't feeling the way I thought I should be on the morning of my final consultation. For starters, everything that could go wrong that morning did. Not the type that felt like obstacles, but more like warnings, so I reluctantly took heed and cancelled everything. Needless to say, I was not happy at all.

I just really wanted to be done with this book. As therapeutic as it's been in so many ways, it feels like a task, having to sit at my bedside with my eyes closed for hours, just so that I can feel, realize, and sort through emotions and events in my life. Things that I would prefer not to share with anyone. I don't enjoy writing this book because it feels like I've been positioned for the enemy's fury. The attacks just keep coming.

As I write these words, I am battling with what now feels like a task — LIVING. I don't want to write about this, even though I vowed to be transparent. I just don't want to deal with this. This feeling and topic has plagued me throughout the entire writing process, but I managed to suppress it, until now. I don't have any more distractions. When and how did dying become more enticing?

At the time I decided to stop the publishing process, I was really busy because I was given the privilege to be the wedding coordinator for my mother's wedding. So naturally, I just channelled all of my energy into the wedding planning. Now that it's all over, everything that I didn't want to acknowledge and shoved to the back burner is now flaring up, and there is no other option left but to face it head on.

A little over a month ago, on the 31st December to be exact, I listened to a woman speak about how she wrestled depression for most of her life. She explained that her "episodes" were sporadic and there were times when she'd be perfectly fine and optimistic for up to two months, and then out of nowhere she would have a mental breakdown.

The more I listened to her, the more engrossed I became. It was as if she had somehow gotten into my head and gathered my personal information and was reading it back to me. The negative emotions, some of the hallucinations, the vicious cycle that she has been a slave to —I've experienced all that she described at some point. She was telling my story. I felt almost vindicated to hear someone else say that she woke up every day and appeared "functional" even though she felt like she was losing her mind and scared because it was only a matter of time before someone noticed. I'm grateful that she shared her story; it touched me in so many ways. I felt relieved, scared, hopeful, and understood, all at the same time.

It was a real eye opener for me when she said that she is a very sensitive person and explained what her triggers were. I grapple with the same triggers (and more) but I never would have used the word sensitive to describe myself. Being sensitive to me meant that you were soft or weak or fragile, all of which I stood against.

I admit that I am easily offended; I get angry for the most ridiculous things. I sometimes think that I'm the topic of everyone's conversations and everything I do and say is being critiqued, so I rehearse everything — my smile, my laugh, my conversations. All in the pursuit of wanting to be enough for everyone. On a rational level, I know that it's unattainable. There is nothing that I could ever do or say that would allow me to reach that level of perfection. But it doesn't keep me from trying to prove myself. Writing this is harder than I thought! I really don't like it but I have to.

Life feels like a burden, because I don't know how to express my emotions without feeling out of control. It's always been easier for me to stuff my pain in, rather than acknowledge it. To show that I am vulnerable, confused or sad is the most petrifying thing for me. But now I have a dilemma. I ran out of storage space, and all of the toxins that I refused to expel along the way have been mixed together and the chemical reaction is killing me slowly from the inside.

I feel like two different people. One knows exactly why and what is happening, and the other is so hopelessly delusional. Some days I wonder, why me? But other days I put my hands up and say, why not me?

You know the saying, "Be careful what you wish for." Well I'm paying for that right now. I thought I was being noble by praying for Yahweh to use me as a vessel to be of service to others. But to be honest, I'm the one who feels like I need all the help that I can get! I feel like I am of no use to myself and certainly not to anyone else but that's the side of me that Yahweh has given the enemy permission to tempt. The other side of me understands that in order to gain trust and genuinely help others in a similar situation, I had to reach the breaking point too. I have to be able to speak their language in order to connect with them, and then trust Yahweh to do the rest.

It's easy to judge when you're not in a situation. I realize everyone's threshold is different, and what might be an easy fix for some, may be overwhelming for others. Sometimes, other factors are at play as well. For example, some days are just difficult to begin with; at least that's how it's been for me. There's a hopelessness that I feel which makes dying an option.

I can't give an explanation that would be justifiable to someone who has never contemplated suicide but as the lyrics in the song 'Not An Easy Road' go, "Who feels it knows." You actually have to be in this fight to truly understand.

I know that I'm alive, but not living. Sometimes it feels like I'm being asphyxiated, so if the option presents itself, why not hasten the process? I hear people saying that they never thought of killing themselves, and all I can say to that is count your blessings.

When they chime in with they never will and they could never be driven to that point, it's as painful as hearing nails on a chalk board. Until you have truly taken a beating from life that has left you limping and scarred, just sitting and hypothesising doesn't qualify you to shoulda, coulda, or woulda anyone else's desperate choices.

One may think that the solution is simple: just go out and live your life. But the strange thing about being in the dark for so long is that every time you see even as much as a glimmer of light, you almost start to miss the darkness because the light hurts. It's painful, it's costly and it's scary but I'm trusting that the pain of walking towards the light is worth more than every scary step that I take.

Father, I come to you weary, weak, and torn in my body and mind. I'm asking for your Holy Spirit to take complete control of everything that pertains to me, but what I need more than anything, is for you to raise the volume of your voice to drown out the screeching of the enemy and apprehend every demand that is on my life. Let your resurrected and redemptive spirit flow through me like never before, because Father you gave me an assignment that threatens every plot of the enemy but I will complete it. Clothe me with your whole armour, for you said that I wrestle not with flesh and blood, but against principalities and powers, rulers of darkness of this world, and against spiritual wickedness in high places. Please give me the grace to stand strong.

Suicidal thoughts were a daily struggle for me, and I attempted suicide twice over the years. The first time I was thirteen years old. It was a Sunday evening and my mother got tickets to a hotel Christmas sale/children's party. All the children were entitled to a gift and snacks, and I was very excited to be attending — up until I got dressed and looked at myself in the mirror. I hated everything about the way I looked.

When I first picked out my outfit, I imagined myself looking slimmer in it, but the reality was very different. So I made up my mind that I wouldn't go. I can't remember what excuse I gave, and my mother tried her best to convince me to go, but it didn't work. My mother and my aunt went, and I was angry because they didn't give in to my tantrum. So I decided that I was going to cause them pain for not trying harder to easy my pain.

I didn't know what to do — all I could come up with was to close all the windows and doors, spray an entire bottle of insecticide in the room, and then sit down and inhale it. Usually the slightest whiff of any chemical causes my eyes to burn and my lips to blister, so I thought certainly an entire bottle will do some serious damage; but on that day, sitting in that room with about three quarts of the bottle sprayed out, the only thing that happened was that

I started to cough, and my grandmother called out to me because she lived next door. Apparently, I forgot the mission because I opened the door to answer her and that was the end of that.

I attempted suicide for the second time when I was twenty-seven years old. I was at my heaviest weight of 350 lbs. and I was depressed. Every time I looked at myself, I saw failure. I had a theme song, "You're fat, ugly and stupid and if you think that any man in his right mind would ever want to marry you, then you're even more stupid than you think." I really wanted to be slim, have a husband, feel secure enough to enjoy time with my friends and do all the other "normal" things that people do, but I was convinced that I'd never get to experience them. That made living this life pointless so I planned to cut my wrists with a pair of scissors that I kept at the side of my bed.

I went back and forth in my mind for a few days but something happened that threw me over the edge. I was walking down the stairs wearing shorts and I heard my inner thighs clap together. The sound shocked me to my core and I thought, "Who the hell body parts makes these sounds just walking down the stairs?" I was done. So I turned right around, went back up the stairs into my bedroom and I looked at my legs in the mirror. I looked at how big and loose they were and how much cellulite I had.

That fuelled me to do it and I said a prayer for my mother. I prayed that Yahweh would strengthen and comfort her. I asked Him to let her know that I loved her and that it was not her fault that I did this, because she tried her best with me and she is an amazing mother.

I must admit that deep inside, I didn't really want to die but I felt like I had to do it. I was never going to experience any form of happiness in this world. Everything was there but not available to me. I felt like I was losing my mind so I laid on my bed, shaking and in tears and lightly passed the scissors over my wrist. I was scared and I paused but then I did it again with a little more force. It wasn't enough to cut my skin, it just scraped me. I paused again and closed my eyes with the intention of doing it for real the next time but I didn't want to see, so I took a deep breath started to ask for forgiveness. The next thing I remember was waking up and outside was dark. The scissors was under me. I remember initially being scared because of what I nearly did and thankful that it didn't happen, but it wasn't long before I was sad again because nothing changed in my life.

Today I am thankful that those two times didn't work and I'm grateful that I have this book so I can vent whenever I start to feel overwhelmed. Writing has also given me a purpose. I feel that I have a responsibility to not only share my story but to pay more attention to people, because many of us are masters of disguise. All those times of despair have prepared me to know when others are pretending that everything is okay with them.

Yahweh, my prayer is that You will use my pain to help others. Suicide and the thoughts of committing suicide is happening every day and is all around, we just don't expect or accept it. The enemy is roaming the earth, seeking those he can devour but Father, You chose me and that means You will not let me lose, even though it feels like I'm being defeated. I will not be defeated, because all the thoughts that You have towards me are of peace and not of evil to give me a hopeful future. I pray that You would keep me in the pocket of humility so that I will always be dependent on You because there is no way I can win without You Father.

I'll continue to seek Yahweh to be made whole because only He has the power to do it. Not money, not power, not friends, not a husband, not losing weight — nothing but Him. I'll admit, His way is not fun, but every other way I've tried to obtain true fulfilment and wholeness has disappointed me. Don't misunderstand me, all of those things are blessings but I shouldn't desire the gifts more than the giver of those gifts.

Most of the time, all I have is faith the size of a mustard seed to trust and believe that the potter (Yahweh) moulds the clay that is my life.

I have lost many battles, more than I can remember. But one thing is for certain, I'm determined to win the war by choosing to believe that all of my battle fields are in a controlled environment, one in which the covenant has fixed my fight. It ain't over till it's over.

**I pray that you and I will always know
that we are fearfully and wonderfully made.
I pray that our Heavenly Father would diffuse**

every planned attack on our lives by the enemy.
When we sin, I pray that we will have enough faith
in our Father to run to him and not listen to the guilt
and condemnation of the enemy.
I pray that our minds would not be conformed to
the things of this world, but renewed by the words
of the All Mighty King.
I pray that we would grow in wisdom,
statue and favour with Yahweh and man.
I pray that on our journey, while the storms rage,
we would dwell in the secret place of the Most High.
I pray that we would have faith enough to be
like Yahshua and go to sleep,
while the winds of life toss our boats back and forth.
Do what you can; Yahweh will take care of the rest.
I ask all this in the name of Yahshua;
thank you for hearing and answering my prayer.

I'm tired of the fantasy island that I've created to spend most of my time away from connecting to the real world. I'm tired of being a recluse, even though I denied it for years. If I had a dollar for every time I heard I'd end up looking just like the walls of my house, I'd be a rich woman. I pretended that I liked being alone but that's a lie. All that did was leave me time to go on the internet and search for people who were feeling the same, which created a comfortable but toxic environment that validated my pity party. No more! I am going to show up for life events.

I know the enemy thought he had me beat, but I was only half-dead, which means there are still possibilities. Yes, I have to dig deep to find them and as much as I don't feel like doing it, I'm doing it anyway — starting with sharing my struggle with suicide, one of the most difficult things that I've ever done.

As long as we decide to serve The Father, none of us is exempt from Satan's schemes. We must expect that the enemy will never stop attacking. It doesn't get any easier either, but I know that every time I pass the test by not giving in to his temptation, I am strengthened for the next time he sets his snares to trap me. The enemy is after one thing and one thing only: to destroy me by any means necessary.

One of the ways he does this is by attacking me in areas where I think that I'm weak. To make it worse, I go out of my way to conceal it, which he loves because he operates in darkness. Basically, what I'm doing is creating a playground for the enemy to play in. Truth is, thanks to Yahweh, I have more strength, favour and grace in those areas and the enemy knows that. I'm the one who doesn't recognize how powerful I am.

The enemy sets traps in places we can't even fathom. We know that he takes pleasure in beating us when we are down, but he will also use the areas where we think we're strong to try and defeat us. It doesn't matter how much we may have sacrificed, he'll concoct a way to use it against us. So we have to challenge ourselves to always keep Yahweh first in all that we do. It has to be intentional because it's easy to become self-reliant and less dependent on Yahweh, which will only decrease our chances of having a relationship with Him. The good news is that Yahweh is always there waiting for us when we awake from the slumber that we sometimes find ourselves in. He is there to love us unconditionally, without judgment. When I think of all the times that I wish I wasn't born or this world would be better without me, the most agonizing thing was my feeling of being unfulfilled. That I had no purpose but that was a lie, birthed out of fear.

False Evidence Appearing Real

"Delay is not denial" and "Every disappointment is for the better" are very powerful expressions and should serve as encouragement in our low moments. But honestly, sometimes I don't like to hear them. When I pray and it isn't answered when or how I want it to be, I don't really want to be encouraged. My disappointment is my justification ticket that grants me entry to the pity party.

But the time has come where I have to start taking responsibility for my choices. I could justify feeling subpar when things don't go my way. I have every right too, as long as I understand that justifying my wrong decisions would only do me more harm than good in the long run. Finding ways to justify my wrong decisions inevitably separate me from the will of Yahweh, which leaves me empty and confused. I believed the lies that the enemy told me for so long. Every lie that he whispered seemed like the only logical solution at the time and produced all my irrational thoughts.

You may be asking yourself, "What qualifies her to write such a book when she clearly isn't a finished work?" Well I beat you to it. I asked myself that very question more times than I could remember. One day, I finally listened to the story about Moses and how Yahweh instructed him to go down into Egypt, and warn the pharaoh to let the descendants of Jacob go free or be destroyed. Moses, a Hebrew, knew about the reputation of the pharaoh in Egypt so he was terrified and almost wanted to disobey Yahweh. He felt insufficient because of his lack of faith and his inability to speak well, so he tried to ask Yahweh to send someone else. But Yahweh still used him and the rest is history! Moses wasn't perfect and Yahweh still chose him to help deliver his people.

I'm still terrified, but that story gave me the inspiration and strength to continue writing this book. I know who I am, logically speaking. I know where I started and what my qualifications are, or the lack thereof for that matter. I choose to believe that greater is He that is in me, than he that is in the world. I have to believe that in spite of all of the opposition, because therein lay the answers. By the grace of Yahweh, I managed to finish this book and my hope is that it would help at least one of you to know that you're not alone.

Keep on trusting in The One who created heaven and earth and take it one uncertain step at a time. He'll see you through, just as He is with me. Like Moses, who seemed the least likely candidate to carry out His task, I also seem like the most unlikely candidate for this job. My vessels are often empty, which is why I read that story over and over for encouragement and validation.

I know how it feels to be broken and what it feels like to be a sinner who deliberately sins and then gets drenched with guilt. It was easy for me to point a finger at others before, but now I feel so much empathy. I pray that it would forever keep me humble, knowing that it's only by His grace that I am able to write these words. I am constantly stumbling, but it's all a part of the walk with Him. I just have to be deliberate in my steps. Even when we let go of His hands, He'll never let go of ours.

**When you'r ready to give birth surround yourself with midwives.
I had no idea what I was doing when I started this process,
but I am blessed to beyond words to have these
two professional and compassionate women willingly
give of their time and expertise.
I'm extremely thankful for your patience.**

EDITOR
Patrice M. Charles

PHOTOGRAPHER
Paula Obe

BOOK LAYOUT
Bamboo Talk Press

Printed in Great Britain
by Amazon